C-4885 CAREER EXAMINATION SERIES

This is your PASSBOOK for...

Developmental Disabilities Program Specialist IV

Test Preparation Study Guide
Questions & Answers

NLC®

NATIONAL LEARNING CORPORATION®

National Learning Corporation

212 Michael Drive, Syosset, NY 11791
(516) 921-8888 • www.passbooks.com
E-mail: info@passbooks.com

PASSBOOK® SERIES

THE *PASSBOOK® SERIES* has been created to prepare applicants and candidates for the ultimate academic battlefield – the examination room.

At some time in our lives, each and every one of us may be required to take an examination – for validation, matriculation, admission, qualification, registration, certification, or licensure.

Based on the assumption that every applicant or candidate has met the basic formal educational standards, has taken the required number of courses, and read the necessary texts, the *PASSBOOK® SERIES* furnishes the one special preparation which may assure passing with confidence, instead of failing with insecurity. Examination questions – together with answers – are furnished as the basic vehicle for study so that the mysteries of the examination and its compounding difficulties may be eliminated or diminished by a sure method.

This book is meant to help you pass your examination provided that you qualify and are serious in your objective.

The entire field is reviewed through the huge store of content information which is succinctly presented through a provocative and challenging approach – the question-and-answer method.

A climate of success is established by furnishing the correct answers at the end of each test.

You soon learn to recognize types of questions, forms of questions, and patterns of questioning. You may even begin to anticipate expected outcomes.

You perceive that many questions are repeated or adapted so that you can gain acute insights, which may enable you to score many sure points.

You learn how to confront new questions, or types of questions, and to attack them confidently and work out the correct answers.

You note objectives and emphases, and recognize pitfalls and dangers, so that you may make positive educational adjustments.

Moreover, you are kept fully informed in relation to new concepts, methods, practices, and directions in the field.

You discover that you are actually taking the examination all the time: you are preparing for the examination by "taking" an examination, not by reading extraneous and/or supererogatory textbooks.

In short, this PASSBOOK®, used directedly, should be an important factor in helping you to pass your test.

DEVELOPMENTAL DISABILITIES PROGRAM SPECIALIST IV

DUTIES:

As a Developmental Disabilities Program Specialist IV, you would direct and coordinate the provision of community-based services to individuals with developmental disabilities. This would include assessing the range of services available to individuals, identifying service gaps, ensuring that appropriate services are developed to address unmet needs, and monitoring the quality of services provided to individuals. You would provide assistance in planning, budget preparation, and regulatory compliance to local governments and private agencies providing services to individuals with disabilities.

SUBJECT OF EXAMINATION:

The written test is designed to test for knowledge, skills, and/or abilities in such areas as:

1. **Working and interacting with others** – These questions test for knowledge of how to effectively approach work and maintain professional relationships with others in the workplace. Each question presents a situation and a number of possible approaches for handling it. Question topics may include working with supervisors and coworkers, interacting with members of the public, handling conflict, and managing workplace demands and priorities. The questions are not specific to any job title or place of work.
2. **Preparing reports and official documents** - These questions test for the ability to prepare reports and other official documents for use within and among governmental agencies, in legal or regulatory settings, or for dissemination to the public. Some questions test for a knowledge of grammar, usage, punctuation, and sentence structure. Others test for the ability to present information clearly and accurately, to use the proper tone, and to organize paragraphs logically and comprehensibly.
3. **Analyzing and evaluating information** - These questions test for the ability to analyze, interpret, and draw reasonable conclusions from information presented in text, data, images or symbols. This may involve identifying a significant problem or issue; focusing on relevant data and text; identifying trends, relationships, and significant features; assessing relevant alternatives; suggesting or evaluating possible conclusions; and applying logical principles to information provided.
4. **Administrative supervision** - These questions test for knowledge of the principles and practices involved in directing the activities of a large subordinate staff, including subordinate supervisors. Questions relate to the personal interactions between an upper level supervisor and his/her subordinate supervisors in the accomplishment of objectives. These questions cover such areas as assigning work to and coordinating the activities of several units, establishing and guiding staff development programs, evaluating the performance of subordinate supervisors, and maintaining relationships with other organizational sections.
5. **Understanding and applying administrative principles** - These questions test for knowledge of how to effectively manage and direct an organization or an organizational segment. These questions cover such areas as developing objectives, formulating policies, making decisions, forecasting and planning, developing personnel, organizing and coordinating work, communicating information, providing leadership, and delegating authority and responsibility.

DEVELOPMENTAL DISABILITIES PROGRAM SPECIALIST IV

[illegible]

HOW TO TAKE A TEST

I. YOU MUST PASS AN EXAMINATION

A. WHAT EVERY CANDIDATE SHOULD KNOW

Examination applicants often ask us for help in preparing for the written test. What can I study in advance? What kinds of questions will be asked? How will the test be given? How will the papers be graded?

As an applicant for a civil service examination, you may be wondering about some of these things. Our purpose here is to suggest effective methods of advance study and to describe civil service examinations.

Your chances for success on this examination can be increased if you know how to prepare. Those "pre-examination jitters" can be reduced if you know what to expect. You can even experience an adventure in good citizenship if you know why civil service exams are given.

B. WHY ARE CIVIL SERVICE EXAMINATIONS GIVEN?

Civil service examinations are important to you in two ways. As a citizen, you want public jobs filled by employees who know how to do their work. As a job seeker, you want a fair chance to compete for that job on an equal footing with other candidates. The best-known means of accomplishing this two-fold goal is the competitive examination.

Exams are widely publicized throughout the nation. They may be administered for jobs in federal, state, city, municipal, town or village governments or agencies.

Any citizen may apply, with some limitations, such as the age or residence of applicants. Your experience and education may be reviewed to see whether you meet the requirements for the particular examination. When these requirements exist, they are reasonable and applied consistently to all applicants. Thus, a competitive examination may cause you some uneasiness now, but it is your privilege and safeguard.

C. HOW ARE CIVIL SERVICE EXAMS DEVELOPED?

Examinations are carefully written by trained technicians who are specialists in the field known as "psychological measurement," in consultation with recognized authorities in the field of work that the test will cover. These experts recommend the subject matter areas or skills to be tested; only those knowledges or skills important to your success on the job are included. The most reliable books and source materials available are used as references. Together, the experts and technicians judge the difficulty level of the questions.

Test technicians know how to phrase questions so that the problem is clearly stated. Their ethics do not permit "trick" or "catch" questions. Questions may have been tried out on sample groups, or subjected to statistical analysis, to determine their usefulness.

Written tests are often used in combination with performance tests, ratings of training and experience, and oral interviews. All of these measures combine to form the best-known means of finding the right person for the right job.

II. HOW TO PASS THE WRITTEN TEST

A. NATURE OF THE EXAMINATION

To prepare intelligently for civil service examinations, you should know how they differ from school examinations you have taken. In school you were assigned certain definite pages to read or subjects to cover. The examination questions were quite detailed and usually emphasized memory. Civil service exams, on the other hand, try to discover your present ability to perform the duties of a position, plus your potentiality to learn these duties. In other words, a civil service exam attempts to predict how successful you will be. Questions cover such a broad area that they cannot be as minute and detailed as school exam questions.

In the public service similar kinds of work, or positions, are grouped together in one "class." This process is known as *position-classification.* All the positions in a class are paid according to the salary range for that class. One class title covers all of these positions, and they are all tested by the same examination.

B. FOUR BASIC STEPS

1) Study the announcement

How, then, can you know what subjects to study? Our best answer is: "Learn as much as possible about the class of positions for which you've applied." The exam will test the knowledge, skills and abilities needed to do the work.

Your most valuable source of information about the position you want is the official exam announcement. This announcement lists the training and experience qualifications. Check these standards and apply only if you come reasonably close to meeting them.

The brief description of the position in the examination announcement offers some clues to the subjects which will be tested. Think about the job itself. Review the duties in your mind. Can you perform them, or are there some in which you are rusty? Fill in the blank spots in your preparation.

Many jurisdictions preview the written test in the exam announcement by including a section called "Knowledge and Abilities Required," "Scope of the Examination," or some similar heading. Here you will find out specifically what fields will be tested.

2) Review your own background

Once you learn in general what the position is all about, and what you need to know to do the work, ask yourself which subjects you already know fairly well and which need improvement. You may wonder whether to concentrate on improving your strong areas or on building some background in your fields of weakness. When the announcement has specified "some knowledge" or "considerable knowledge," or has used adjectives like "beginning principles of..." or "advanced ... methods," you can get a clue as to the number and difficulty of questions to be asked in any given field. More questions, and hence broader coverage, would be included for those subjects which are more important in the work. Now weigh your strengths and weaknesses against the job requirements and prepare accordingly.

3) Determine the level of the position

Another way to tell how intensively you should prepare is to understand the level of the job for which you are applying. Is it the entering level? In other words, is this the position in which beginners in a field of work are hired? Or is it an intermediate or advanced level? Sometimes this is indicated by such words as "Junior" or "Senior" in the class title. Other jurisdictions use Roman numerals to designate the level – Clerk I, Clerk II, for example. The word "Supervisor" sometimes appears in the title. If the level is not indicated by the title, check the description of duties. Will you be working under very close supervision, or will you have responsibility for independent decisions in this work?

4) Choose appropriate study materials

Now that you know the subjects to be examined and the relative amount of each subject to be covered, you can choose suitable study materials. For beginning level jobs, or even advanced ones, if you have a pronounced weakness in some aspect of your training, read a modern, standard textbook in that field. Be sure it is up to date and has general coverage. Such books are normally available at your library, and the librarian will be glad to help you locate one. For entry-level positions, questions of appropriate difficulty are chosen – neither highly advanced questions, nor those too simple. Such questions require careful thought but not advanced training.

If the position for which you are applying is technical or advanced, you will read more advanced, specialized material. If you are already familiar with the basic principles of your field, elementary textbooks would waste your time. Concentrate on advanced textbooks and technical periodicals. Think through the concepts and review difficult problems in your field.

These are all general sources. You can get more ideas on your own initiative, following these leads. For example, training manuals and publications of the government agency which employs workers in your field can be useful, particularly for technical and professional positions. A letter or visit to the government department involved may result in more specific study suggestions, and certainly will provide you with a more definite idea of the exact nature of the position you are seeking.

III. KINDS OF TESTS

Tests are used for purposes other than measuring knowledge and ability to perform specified duties. For some positions, it is equally important to test ability to make adjustments to new situations or to profit from training. In others, basic mental abilities not dependent on information are essential. Questions which test these things may not appear as pertinent to the duties of the position as those which test for knowledge and information. Yet they are often highly important parts of a fair examination. For very general questions, it is almost impossible to help you direct your study efforts. What we can do is to point out some of the more common of these general abilities needed in public service positions and describe some typical questions.

1) General information

Broad, general information has been found useful for predicting job success in some kinds of work. This is tested in a variety of ways, from vocabulary lists to questions about current events. Basic background in some field of work, such as sociology or economics, may be sampled in a group of questions. Often these are principles which have become familiar to most persons through exposure rather than through formal training. It is difficult to advise you how to study for these questions; being alert to the world around you is our best suggestion.

2) Verbal ability

An example of an ability needed in many positions is verbal or language ability. Verbal ability is, in brief, the ability to use and understand words. Vocabulary and grammar tests are typical measures of this ability. Reading comprehension or paragraph interpretation questions are common in many kinds of civil service tests. You are given a paragraph of written material and asked to find its central meaning.

3) Numerical ability

Number skills can be tested by the familiar arithmetic problem, by checking paired lists of numbers to see which are alike and which are different, or by interpreting charts and graphs. In the latter test, a graph may be printed in the test booklet which you are asked to use as the basis for answering questions.

4) Observation

A popular test for law-enforcement positions is the observation test. A picture is shown to you for several minutes, then taken away. Questions about the picture test your ability to observe both details and larger elements.

5) Following directions

In many positions in the public service, the employee must be able to carry out written instructions dependably and accurately. You may be given a chart with several columns, each column listing a variety of information. The questions require you to carry out directions involving the information given in the chart.

6) Skills and aptitudes

Performance tests effectively measure some manual skills and aptitudes. When the skill is one in which you are trained, such as typing or shorthand, you can practice. These tests are often very much like those given in business school or high school courses. For many of the other skills and aptitudes, however, no short-time preparation can be made. Skills and abilities natural to you or that you have developed throughout your lifetime are being tested.

Many of the general questions just described provide all the data needed to answer the questions and ask you to use your reasoning ability to find the answers. Your best preparation for these tests, as well as for tests of facts and ideas, is to be at your physical and mental best. You, no doubt, have your own methods of getting into an exam-taking mood and keeping "in shape." The next section lists some ideas on this subject.

IV. KINDS OF QUESTIONS

Only rarely is the "essay" question, which you answer in narrative form, used in civil service tests. Civil service tests are usually of the short-answer type. Full instructions for answering these questions will be given to you at the examination. But in case this is your first experience with short-answer questions and separate answer sheets, here is what you need to know:

1) Multiple-choice Questions

Most popular of the short-answer questions is the "multiple choice" or "best answer" question. It can be used, for example, to test for factual knowledge, ability to solve problems or judgment in meeting situations found at work.

A multiple-choice question is normally one of three types—

- It can begin with an incomplete statement followed by several possible endings. You are to find the one ending which *best* completes the statement, although some of the others may not be entirely wrong.
- It can also be a complete statement in the form of a question which is answered by choosing one of the statements listed.

- It can be in the form of a problem – again you select the best answer.

Here is an example of a multiple-choice question with a discussion which should give you some clues as to the method for choosing the right answer:

When an employee has a complaint about his assignment, the action which will *best* help him overcome his difficulty is to
A. discuss his difficulty with his coworkers
B. take the problem to the head of the organization
C. take the problem to the person who gave him the assignment
D. say nothing to anyone about his complaint

In answering this question, you should study each of the choices to find which is best. Consider choice "A" – Certainly an employee may discuss his complaint with fellow employees, but no change or improvement can result, and the complaint remains unresolved. Choice "B" is a poor choice since the head of the organization probably does not know what assignment you have been given, and taking your problem to him is known as "going over the head" of the supervisor. The supervisor, or person who made the assignment, is the person who can clarify it or correct any injustice. Choice "C" is, therefore, correct. To say nothing, as in choice "D," is unwise. Supervisors have and interest in knowing the problems employees are facing, and the employee is seeking a solution to his problem.

2) True/False Questions

The "true/false" or "right/wrong" form of question is sometimes used. Here a complete statement is given. Your job is to decide whether the statement is right or wrong.

SAMPLE: A roaming cell-phone call to a nearby city costs less than a non-roaming call to a distant city.

This statement is wrong, or false, since roaming calls are more expensive.

This is not a complete list of all possible question forms, although most of the others are variations of these common types. You will always get complete directions for answering questions. Be sure you understand *how* to mark your answers – ask questions until you do.

V. RECORDING YOUR ANSWERS

Computer terminals are used more and more today for many different kinds of exams.

For an examination with very few applicants, you may be told to record your answers in the test booklet itself. Separate answer sheets are much more common. If this separate answer sheet is to be scored by machine – and this is often the case – it is highly important that you mark your answers correctly in order to get credit.

An electronic scoring machine is often used in civil service offices because of the speed with which papers can be scored. Machine-scored answer sheets must be marked with a pencil, which will be given to you. This pencil has a high graphite content which responds to the electronic scoring machine. As a matter of fact, stray dots may register as answers, so do not let your pencil rest on the answer sheet while you are pondering the correct answer. Also, if your pencil lead breaks or is otherwise defective, ask for another.

Since the answer sheet will be dropped in a slot in the scoring machine, be careful not to bend the corners or get the paper crumpled.

The answer sheet normally has five vertical columns of numbers, with 30 numbers to a column. These numbers correspond to the question numbers in your test booklet. After each number, going across the page are four or five pairs of dotted lines. These short dotted lines have small letters or numbers above them. The first two pairs may also have a "T" or "F" above the letters. This indicates that the first two pairs only are to be used if the questions are of the true-false type. If the questions are multiple choice, disregard the "T" and "F" and pay attention only to the small letters or numbers.

Answer your questions in the manner of the sample that follows:

32. The largest city in the United States is
    A. Washington, D.C.
    B. New York City
    C. Chicago
    D. Detroit
    E. San Francisco

1) Choose the answer you think is best. (New York City is the largest, so "B" is correct.)
2) Find the row of dotted lines numbered the same as the question you are answering. (Find row number 32)
3) Find the pair of dotted lines corresponding to the answer. (Find the pair of lines under the mark "B.")
4) Make a solid black mark between the dotted lines.

VI. BEFORE THE TEST

Common sense will help you find procedures to follow to get ready for an examination. Too many of us, however, overlook these sensible measures. Indeed, nervousness and fatigue have been found to be the most serious reasons why applicants fail to do their best on civil service tests. Here is a list of reminders:

- Begin your preparation early – Don't wait until the last minute to go scurrying around for books and materials or to find out what the position is all about.
- Prepare continuously – An hour a night for a week is better than an all-night cram session. This has been definitely established. What is more, a night a week for a month will return better dividends than crowding your study into a shorter period of time.
- Locate the place of the exam – You have been sent a notice telling you when and where to report for the examination. If the location is in a different town or otherwise unfamiliar to you, it would be well to inquire the best route and learn something about the building.
- Relax the night before the test – Allow your mind to rest. Do not study at all that night. Plan some mild recreation or diversion; then go to bed early and get a good night's sleep.
- Get up early enough to make a leisurely trip to the place for the test – This way unforeseen events, traffic snarls, unfamiliar buildings, etc. will not upset you.
- Dress comfortably – A written test is not a fashion show. You will be known by number and not by name, so wear something comfortable.

- Leave excess paraphernalia at home – Shopping bags and odd bundles will get in your way. You need bring only the items mentioned in the official notice you received; usually everything you need is provided. Do not bring reference books to the exam. They will only confuse those last minutes and be taken away from you when in the test room.
- Arrive somewhat ahead of time – If because of transportation schedules you must get there very early, bring a newspaper or magazine to take your mind off yourself while waiting.
- Locate the examination room – When you have found the proper room, you will be directed to the seat or part of the room where you will sit. Sometimes you are given a sheet of instructions to read while you are waiting. Do not fill out any forms until you are told to do so; just read them and be prepared.
- Relax and prepare to listen to the instructions
- If you have any physical problem that may keep you from doing your best, be sure to tell the test administrator. If you are sick or in poor health, you really cannot do your best on the exam. You can come back and take the test some other time.

VII. AT THE TEST

The day of the test is here and you have the test booklet in your hand. The temptation to get going is very strong. Caution! There is more to success than knowing the right answers. You must know how to identify your papers and understand variations in the type of short-answer question used in this particular examination. Follow these suggestions for maximum results from your efforts:

1) Cooperate with the monitor

The test administrator has a duty to create a situation in which you can be as much at ease as possible. He will give instructions, tell you when to begin, check to see that you are marking your answer sheet correctly, and so on. He is not there to guard you, although he will see that your competitors do not take unfair advantage. He wants to help you do your best.

2) Listen to all instructions

Don't jump the gun! Wait until you understand all directions. In most civil service tests you get more time than you need to answer the questions. So don't be in a hurry. Read each word of instructions until you clearly understand the meaning. Study the examples, listen to all announcements and follow directions. Ask questions if you do not understand what to do.

3) Identify your papers

Civil service exams are usually identified by number only. You will be assigned a number; you must not put your name on your test papers. Be sure to copy your number correctly. Since more than one exam may be given, copy your exact examination title.

4) Plan your time

Unless you are told that a test is a "speed" or "rate of work" test, speed itself is usually not important. Time enough to answer all the questions will be provided, but this does not mean that you have all day. An overall time limit has been set. Divide the total time (in minutes) by the number of questions to determine the approximate time you have for each question.

5) Do not linger over difficult questions

If you come across a difficult question, mark it with a paper clip (useful to have along) and come back to it when you have been through the booklet. One caution if you do this – be sure to skip a number on your answer sheet as well. Check often to be sure that you have not lost your place and that you are marking in the row numbered the same as the question you are answering.

6) Read the questions

Be sure you know what the question asks! Many capable people are unsuccessful because they failed to *read* the questions correctly.

7) Answer all questions

Unless you have been instructed that a penalty will be deducted for incorrect answers, it is better to guess than to omit a question.

8) Speed tests

It is often better NOT to guess on speed tests. It has been found that on timed tests people are tempted to spend the last few seconds before time is called in marking answers at random – without even reading them – in the hope of picking up a few extra points. To discourage this practice, the instructions may warn you that your score will be "corrected" for guessing. That is, a penalty will be applied. The incorrect answers will be deducted from the correct ones, or some other penalty formula will be used.

9) Review your answers

If you finish before time is called, go back to the questions you guessed or omitted to give them further thought. Review other answers if you have time.

10) Return your test materials

If you are ready to leave before others have finished or time is called, take ALL your materials to the monitor and leave quietly. Never take any test material with you. The monitor can discover whose papers are not complete, and taking a test booklet may be grounds for disqualification.

VIII. EXAMINATION TECHNIQUES

1) Read the general instructions carefully. These are usually printed on the first page of the exam booklet. As a rule, these instructions refer to the timing of the examination; the fact that you should not start work until the signal and must stop work at a signal, etc. If there are any *special* instructions, such as a choice of questions to be answered, make sure that you note this instruction carefully.

2) When you are ready to start work on the examination, that is as soon as the signal has been given, read the instructions to each question booklet, underline any key words or phrases, such as *least*, *best*, *outline*, *describe* and the like. In this way you will tend to answer as requested rather than discover on reviewing your paper that you *listed without describing*, that you selected the *worst* choice rather than the *best* choice, etc.

3) If the examination is of the objective or multiple-choice type – that is, each question will also give a series of possible answers: A, B, C or D, and you are called upon to select the best answer and write the letter next to that answer on your answer paper – it is advisable to start answering each question in turn. There may be anywhere from 50 to 100 such questions in the three or four hours allotted and you can see how much time would be taken if you read through all the questions before beginning to answer any. Furthermore, if you come across a question or group of questions which you know would be difficult to answer, it would undoubtedly affect your handling of all the other questions.

4) If the examination is of the essay type and contains but a few questions, it is a moot point as to whether you should read all the questions before starting to answer any one. Of course, if you are given a choice – say five out of seven and the like – then it is essential to read all the questions so you can eliminate the two that are most difficult. If, however, you are asked to answer all the questions, there may be danger in trying to answer the easiest one first because you may find that you will spend too much time on it. The best technique is to answer the first question, then proceed to the second, etc.

5) Time your answers. Before the exam begins, write down the time it started, then add the time allowed for the examination and write down the time it must be completed, then divide the time available somewhat as follows:
   - If 3-1/2 hours are allowed, that would be 210 minutes. If you have 80 objective-type questions, that would be an average of 2-1/2 minutes per question. Allow yourself no more than 2 minutes per question, or a total of 160 minutes, which will permit about 50 minutes to review.
   - If for the time allotment of 210 minutes there are 7 essay questions to answer, that would average about 30 minutes a question. Give yourself only 25 minutes per question so that you have about 35 minutes to review.

6) The most important instruction is to *read each question* and make sure you know what is wanted. The second most important instruction is to *time yourself properly* so that you answer every question. The third most important instruction is to *answer every question.* Guess if you have to but include something for each question. Remember that you will receive no credit for a blank and will probably receive some credit if you write something in answer to an essay question. If you guess a letter – say "B" for a multiple-choice question – you may have guessed right. If you leave a blank as an answer to a multiple-choice question, the examiners may respect your feelings but it will not add a point to your score. Some exams may penalize you for wrong answers, so in such cases *only*, you may not want to guess unless you have some basis for your answer.

7) Suggestions
   a. Objective-type questions
      1. Examine the question booklet for proper sequence of pages and questions
      2. Read all instructions carefully
      3. Skip any question which seems too difficult; return to it after all other questions have been answered
      4. Apportion your time properly; do not spend too much time on any single question or group of questions

5. Note and underline key words – *all, most, fewest, least, best, worst, same, opposite,* etc.
6. Pay particular attention to negatives
7. Note unusual option, e.g., unduly long, short, complex, different or similar in content to the body of the question
8. Observe the use of "hedging" words – *probably, may, most likely,* etc.
9. Make sure that your answer is put next to the same number as the question
10. Do not second-guess unless you have good reason to believe the second answer is definitely more correct
11. Cross out original answer if you decide another answer is more accurate; do not erase until you are ready to hand your paper in
12. Answer all questions; guess unless instructed otherwise
13. Leave time for review

b. Essay questions
1. Read each question carefully
2. Determine exactly what is wanted. Underline key words or phrases.
3. Decide on outline or paragraph answer
4. Include many different points and elements unless asked to develop any one or two points or elements
5. Show impartiality by giving pros and cons unless directed to select one side only
6. Make and write down any assumptions you find necessary to answer the questions
7. Watch your English, grammar, punctuation and choice of words
8. Time your answers; don't crowd material

8) Answering the essay question

Most essay questions can be answered by framing the specific response around several key words or ideas. Here are a few such key words or ideas:

M's: manpower, materials, methods, money, management
P's: purpose, program, policy, plan, procedure, practice, problems, pitfalls, personnel, public relations

a. Six basic steps in handling problems:
1. Preliminary plan and background development
2. Collect information, data and facts
3. Analyze and interpret information, data and facts
4. Analyze and develop solutions as well as make recommendations
5. Prepare report and sell recommendations
6. Install recommendations and follow up effectiveness

b. Pitfalls to avoid
1. *Taking things for granted* – A statement of the situation does not necessarily imply that each of the elements is necessarily true; for example, a complaint may be invalid and biased so that all that can be taken for granted is that a complaint has been registered

2. *Considering only one side of a situation* – Wherever possible, indicate several alternatives and then point out the reasons you selected the best one
3. *Failing to indicate follow up* – Whenever your answer indicates action on your part, make certain that you will take proper follow-up action to see how successful your recommendations, procedures or actions turn out to be
4. *Taking too long in answering any single question* – Remember to time your answers properly

IX. AFTER THE TEST

Scoring procedures differ in detail among civil service jurisdictions although the general principles are the same. Whether the papers are hand-scored or graded by machine we have described, they are nearly always graded by number. That is, the person who marks the paper knows only the number – never the name – of the applicant. Not until all the papers have been graded will they be matched with names. If other tests, such as training and experience or oral interview ratings have been given, scores will be combined. Different parts of the examination usually have different weights. For example, the written test might count 60 percent of the final grade, and a rating of training and experience 40 percent. In many jurisdictions, veterans will have a certain number of points added to their grades.

After the final grade has been determined, the names are placed in grade order and an eligible list is established. There are various methods for resolving ties between those who get the same final grade – probably the most common is to place first the name of the person whose application was received first. Job offers are made from the eligible list in the order the names appear on it. You will be notified of your grade and your rank as soon as all these computations have been made. This will be done as rapidly as possible.

People who are found to meet the requirements in the announcement are called "eligibles." Their names are put on a list of eligible candidates. An eligible's chances of getting a job depend on how high he stands on this list and how fast agencies are filling jobs from the list.

When a job is to be filled from a list of eligibles, the agency asks for the names of people on the list of eligibles for that job. When the civil service commission receives this request, it sends to the agency the names of the three people highest on this list. Or, if the job to be filled has specialized requirements, the office sends the agency the names of the top three persons who meet these requirements from the general list.

The appointing officer makes a choice from among the three people whose names were sent to him. If the selected person accepts the appointment, the names of the others are put back on the list to be considered for future openings.

That is the rule in hiring from all kinds of eligible lists, whether they are for typist, carpenter, chemist, or something else. For every vacancy, the appointing officer has his choice of any one of the top three eligibles on the list. This explains why the person whose name is on top of the list sometimes does not get an appointment when some of the persons lower on the list do. If the appointing officer chooses the second or third eligible, the No. 1 eligible does not get a job at once, but stays on the list until he is appointed or the list is terminated.

X. HOW TO PASS THE INTERVIEW TEST

The examination for which you applied requires an oral interview test. You have already taken the written test and you are now being called for the interview test – the final part of the formal examination.

You may think that it is not possible to prepare for an interview test and that there are no procedures to follow during an interview. Our purpose is to point out some things you can do in advance that will help you and some good rules to follow and pitfalls to avoid while you are being interviewed.

What is an interview supposed to test?

The written examination is designed to test the technical knowledge and competence of the candidate; the oral is designed to evaluate intangible qualities, not readily measured otherwise, and to establish a list showing the relative fitness of each candidate – as measured against his competitors – for the position sought. Scoring is not on the basis of "right" and "wrong," but on a sliding scale of values ranging from "not passable" to "outstanding." As a matter of fact, it is possible to achieve a relatively low score without a single "incorrect" answer because of evident weakness in the qualities being measured.

Occasionally, an examination may consist entirely of an oral test – either an individual or a group oral. In such cases, information is sought concerning the technical knowledges and abilities of the candidate, since there has been no written examination for this purpose. More commonly, however, an oral test is used to supplement a written examination.

Who conducts interviews?

The composition of oral boards varies among different jurisdictions. In nearly all, a representative of the personnel department serves as chairman. One of the members of the board may be a representative of the department in which the candidate would work. In some cases, "outside experts" are used, and, frequently, a businessman or some other representative of the general public is asked to serve. Labor and management or other special groups may be represented. The aim is to secure the services of experts in the appropriate field.

However the board is composed, it is a good idea (and not at all improper or unethical) to ascertain in advance of the interview who the members are and what groups they represent. When you are introduced to them, you will have some idea of their backgrounds and interests, and at least you will not stutter and stammer over their names.

What should be done before the interview?

While knowledge about the board members is useful and takes some of the surprise element out of the interview, there is other preparation which is more substantive. It *is* possible to prepare for an oral interview – in several ways:

1) Keep a copy of your application and review it carefully before the interview

This may be the only document before the oral board, and the starting point of the interview. Know what education and experience you have listed there, and the sequence and dates of all of it. Sometimes the board will ask you to review the highlights of your experience for them; you should not have to hem and haw doing it.

2) Study the class specification and the examination announcement

Usually, the oral board has one or both of these to guide them. The qualities, characteristics or knowledges required by the position sought are stated in these documents. They offer valuable clues as to the nature of the oral interview. For example, if the job involves supervisory responsibilities, the announcement will usually indicate that knowledge of modern supervisory methods and the qualifications of the candidate as a supervisor will be tested. If so, you can expect such questions, frequently in the form of a hypothetical situation which you are expected to solve. NEVER go into an oral without knowledge of the duties and responsibilities of the job you seek.

3) Think through each qualification required

Try to visualize the kind of questions you would ask if you were a board member. How well could you answer them? Try especially to appraise your own knowledge and background in each area, *measured against the job sought*, and identify any areas in which you are weak. Be critical and realistic – do not flatter yourself.

4) Do some general reading in areas in which you feel you may be weak

For example, if the job involves supervision and your past experience has NOT, some general reading in supervisory methods and practices, particularly in the field of human relations, might be useful. Do NOT study agency procedures or detailed manuals. The oral board will be testing your understanding and capacity, not your memory.

5) Get a good night's sleep and watch your general health and mental attitude

You will want a clear head at the interview. Take care of a cold or any other minor ailment, and of course, no hangovers.

What should be done on the day of the interview?

Now comes the day of the interview itself. Give yourself plenty of time to get there. Plan to arrive somewhat ahead of the scheduled time, particularly if your appointment is in the fore part of the day. If a previous candidate fails to appear, the board might be ready for you a bit early. By early afternoon an oral board is almost invariably behind schedule if there are many candidates, and you may have to wait. Take along a book or magazine to read, or your application to review, but leave any extraneous material in the waiting room when you go in for your interview. In any event, relax and compose yourself.

The matter of dress is important. The board is forming impressions about you – from your experience, your manners, your attitude, and your appearance. Give your personal appearance careful attention. Dress your best, but not your flashiest. Choose conservative, appropriate clothing, and be sure it is immaculate. This is a business interview, and your appearance should indicate that you regard it as such. Besides, being well groomed and properly dressed will help boost your confidence.

Sooner or later, someone will call your name and escort you into the interview room. *This is it.* From here on you are on your own. It is too late for any more preparation. But remember, you asked for this opportunity to prove your fitness, and you are here because your request was granted.

What happens when you go in?

The usual sequence of events will be as follows: The clerk (who is often the board stenographer) will introduce you to the chairman of the oral board, who will introduce you to the other members of the board. Acknowledge the introductions before you sit down. Do not be surprised if you find a microphone facing you or a stenotypist sitting by. Oral interviews are usually recorded in the event of an appeal or other review.

Usually the chairman of the board will open the interview by reviewing the highlights of your education and work experience from your application – primarily for the benefit of the other members of the board, as well as to get the material into the record. Do not interrupt or comment unless there is an error or significant misinterpretation; if that is the case, do not hesitate. But do not quibble about insignificant matters. Also, he will usually ask you some question about your education, experience or your present job – partly to get you to start talking and to establish the interviewing "rapport." He may start the actual questioning, or turn it over to one of the other members. Frequently, each member undertakes the questioning on a particular area, one in which he is perhaps most competent, so you can expect each member to participate in the examination. Because time is limited, you may also expect some rather abrupt switches in the direction the questioning takes, so do not be upset by it. Normally, a board member will not pursue a single line of questioning unless he discovers a particular strength or weakness.

After each member has participated, the chairman will usually ask whether any member has any further questions, then will ask you if you have anything you wish to add. Unless you are expecting this question, it may floor you. Worse, it may start you off on an extended, extemporaneous speech. The board is not usually seeking more information. The question is principally to offer you a last opportunity to present further qualifications or to indicate that you have nothing to add. So, if you feel that a significant qualification or characteristic has been overlooked, it is proper to point it out in a sentence or so. Do not compliment the board on the thoroughness of their examination – they have been sketchy, and you know it. If you wish, merely say, "No thank you, I have nothing further to add." This is a point where you can "talk yourself out" of a good impression or fail to present an important bit of information. Remember, *you close the interview yourself.*

The chairman will then say, "That is all, Mr. _______, thank you." Do not be startled; the interview is over, and quicker than you think. Thank him, gather your belongings and take your leave. Save your sigh of relief for the other side of the door.

How to put your best foot forward

Throughout this entire process, you may feel that the board individually and collectively is trying to pierce your defenses, seek out your hidden weaknesses and embarrass and confuse you. Actually, this is not true. They are obliged to make an appraisal of your qualifications for the job you are seeking, and they want to see you in your best light. Remember, they must interview all candidates and a non-cooperative candidate may become a failure in spite of their best efforts to bring out his qualifications. Here are 15 suggestions that will help you:

1) Be natural – Keep your attitude confident, not cocky

If you are not confident that you can do the job, do not expect the board to be. Do not apologize for your weaknesses, try to bring out your strong points. The board is interested in a positive, not negative, presentation. Cockiness will antagonize any board member and make him wonder if you are covering up a weakness by a false show of strength.

2) Get comfortable, but don't lounge or sprawl

Sit erectly but not stiffly. A careless posture may lead the board to conclude that you are careless in other things, or at least that you are not impressed by the importance of the occasion. Either conclusion is natural, even if incorrect. Do not fuss with your clothing, a pencil or an ashtray. Your hands may occasionally be useful to emphasize a point; do not let them become a point of distraction.

3) Do not wisecrack or make small talk

This is a serious situation, and your attitude should show that you consider it as such. Further, the time of the board is limited – they do not want to waste it, and neither should you.

4) Do not exaggerate your experience or abilities

In the first place, from information in the application or other interviews and sources, the board may know more about you than you think. Secondly, you probably will not get away with it. An experienced board is rather adept at spotting such a situation, so do not take the chance.

5) If you know a board member, do not make a point of it, yet do not hide it

Certainly you are not fooling him, and probably not the other members of the board. Do not try to take advantage of your acquaintanceship – it will probably do you little good.

6) Do not dominate the interview

Let the board do that. They will give you the clues – do not assume that you have to do all the talking. Realize that the board has a number of questions to ask you, and do not try to take up all the interview time by showing off your extensive knowledge of the answer to the first one.

7) Be attentive

You only have 20 minutes or so, and you should keep your attention at its sharpest throughout. When a member is addressing a problem or question to you, give him your undivided attention. Address your reply principally to him, but do not exclude the other board members.

8) Do not interrupt

A board member may be stating a problem for you to analyze. He will ask you a question when the time comes. Let him state the problem, and wait for the question.

9) Make sure you understand the question

Do not try to answer until you are sure what the question is. If it is not clear, restate it in your own words or ask the board member to clarify it for you. However, do not haggle about minor elements.

10) Reply promptly but not hastily

A common entry on oral board rating sheets is "candidate responded readily," or "candidate hesitated in replies." Respond as promptly and quickly as you can, but do not jump to a hasty, ill-considered answer.

11) Do not be peremptory in your answers

A brief answer is proper – but do not fire your answer back. That is a losing game from your point of view. The board member can probably ask questions much faster than you can answer them.

12) Do not try to create the answer you think the board member wants

He is interested in what kind of mind you have and how it works – not in playing games. Furthermore, he can usually spot this practice and will actually grade you down on it.

13) Do not switch sides in your reply merely to agree with a board member

Frequently, a member will take a contrary position merely to draw you out and to see if you are willing and able to defend your point of view. Do not start a debate, yet do not surrender a good position. If a position is worth taking, it is worth defending.

14) Do not be afraid to admit an error in judgment if you are shown to be wrong

The board knows that you are forced to reply without any opportunity for careful consideration. Your answer may be demonstrably wrong. If so, admit it and get on with the interview.

15) Do not dwell at length on your present job

The opening question may relate to your present assignment. Answer the question but do not go into an extended discussion. You are being examined for a *new* job, not your present one. As a matter of fact, try to phrase ALL your answers in terms of the job for which you are being examined.

Basis of Rating

Probably you will forget most of these "do's" and "don'ts" when you walk into the oral interview room. Even remembering them all will not ensure you a passing grade. Perhaps you did not have the qualifications in the first place. But remembering them will help you to put your best foot forward, without treading on the toes of the board members.

Rumor and popular opinion to the contrary notwithstanding, an oral board wants you to make the best appearance possible. They know you are under pressure – but they also want to see how you respond to it as a guide to what your reaction would be under the pressures of the job you seek. They will be influenced by the degree of poise you display, the personal traits you show and the manner in which you respond.

ABOUT THIS BOOK

This book contains tests divided into Examination Sections. Go through each test, answering every question in the margin. We have also attached a sample answer sheet at the back of the book that can be removed and used. At the end of each test look at the answer key and check your answers. On the ones you got wrong, look at the right answer choice and learn. Do not fill in the answers first. Do not memorize the questions and answers, but understand the answer and principles involved. On your test, the questions will likely be different from the samples. Questions are changed and new ones added. If you understand these past questions you should have success with any changes that arise. Tests may consist of several types of questions. We have additional books on each subject should more study be advisable or necessary for you. Finally, the more you study, the better prepared you will be. This book is intended to be the last thing you study before you walk into the examination room. Prior study of relevant texts is also recommended. NLC publishes some of these in our Fundamental Series. Knowledge and good sense are important factors in passing your exam. Good luck also helps. So now study this Passbook, absorb the material contained within and take that knowledge into the examination. Then do your best to pass that exam.

EXAMINATION SECTION

EXAMINATION SECTION

TEST 1

DIRECTIONS: Each question or incomplete statement is followed by several suggested answers or completions. Select the one that BEST answers the question or completes the statement. *PRINT THE LETTER OF THE CORRECT ANSWER IN THE SPACE AT THE RIGHT.*

1. In public agencies, communications should be based PRIMARILY on a 1.____
   A. two-way flow from the top down and from the bottom up, most of which should be given in writing to avoid ambiguity
   B. multi-direction flow among all levels and with outside persons
   C. rapid, internal one-way flow from the top down
   D. two-way flow of information, most of which should be given orally for purposes of clarity

2. In some organizations, changes in policy or procedures are often communicated by word of mouth from supervisors to employees with no prior discussion or exchange of viewpoints with employees. 2.____
   This procedure often produces employee dissatisfaction CHIEFLY because
   A. information is mostly unusable since a considerable amount of time is required to transmit information
   B. lower-level supervisors tend to be excessively concerned with minor details
   C. management has failed to seek employees' advice before making changes
   D. valuable staff time is lost between decision-making and the implementation of decisions

3. For good letter writing, you should try to visualize the person to whom you are writing, especially if you know him. 3.____
   Of the following rules, it is LEAST helpful in such visualization to think of
   A. the person's likes and dislikes, his concerns, and his needs
   B. what you would be likely to say if speaking in person
   C. what you would expect to be asked if speaking in person
   D. your official position in order to be certain that your words are proper

4. One approach to good informal letter writing is to make letters and conversational. 4.____
   All of the following practices will usually help to do this EXCEPT:
   A. If possible, use a style which is similar to the style used when speaking
   B. Substitute phrases for single words (e.g., *at the present time for now*)
   C. Use contractions of words (e.g., *you're* for *you are*)
   D. Use ordinary vocabulary when possible

5. All of the following rules will aid in producing clarity in report-writing EXCEPT: 5.____
   A. Give specific details or examples, if possible
   B. Keep related words close together in each sentence
   C. Present information in sequential order
   D. Put several thoughts or ideas in each paragraph

6. The one of the following statements about public relations which is MOST accurate is that 6.____
   A. in the long run, appearance gains better results than performance
   B. objectivity is decreased if outside public relations consultants are employed
   C. public relations is the responsibility of every employee
   D. public relations should be based on a formal publicity program

7. The form of communication which is usually considered to be MOST personally directed to the intended recipient is the 7.____
   A. brochure B. film C. letter D. radio

8. In general, a document that presents an organization's views or opinions on a particular topic is MOST accurately known as a 8.____
   A. tear sheet B. position paper
   C. flyer D. journal

9. Assume that you have been asked to speak before an organization of persons who oppose a newly announced program in which you are involved. You feel tense about talking to this group. 9.____
   Which of the following rules generally would be MOST useful in gaining rapport when speaking before the audience?
   A. Impress them with your experience
   B. Stress all areas of disagreement
   C. Talk to the group as to one person
   D. Use formal grammar and language

10. An organization must have an effective public relations program since, at its best, public relations is a bridge to change. 10.____
   All of the following statements about communication and human behavior have validity EXCEPT:
   A. People are more likely to talk about controversial matters with like-minded people than with those holding other views
   B. The earlier an experience, the more powerful its effect since it influences how later experiences will be interpreted
   C. In periods of social tension, official sources gain increased believability
   D. Those who are already interested in a topic are the ones who are most open to receive new communications about it

11. An employee should be encouraged to talk easily and frankly when he is dealing with his supervisor. 11.____
In order to encourage such free communication, it would be MOST appropriate for a supervisor to behave in a(n)
   A. sincere manner; assure the employee that you will deal with him honestly and openly
   B. official manner; you are a supervisor and must always act formally with subordinates
   C. investigative manner; you must probe and question to get to a basis of trust
   D. unemotional manner; the employee's emotions and background should play no part in your dealings with him

12. Research findings show that an increase in free communication within an agency GENERALLY results in which one of the following? 12.____
   A. Improved morale and productivity
   B. Increased promotional opportunities
   C. An increase in authority
   D. A spirit of honesty

13. Assume that you are a supervisor and your superiors have given you a new-type procedure to be followed. 13.____
Before passing this information on to your subordinates, the one of the following actions that you should take FIRST is to
   A. ask your superiors to send out a memorandum to the entire staff
   B. clarify the procedure in your own mind
   C. set up a training course to provide instruction on the new procedure
   D. write a memorandum to your subordinates

14. Communication is necessary for an organization to be effective. 14.____
The one of the following which is LEAST important for most communication systems is that
   A. messages are sent quickly and directly to the person who needs them to operate
   B. information should be conveyed understandably and accurately
   C. the method used to transmit information should be kept secret so that security can be maintained
   D. senders of messages must know how their messages are received and acted upon

15. Which one of the following is the CHIEF advantage of listening willingly to subordinates and encouraging them to talk freely and honestly? 15.____
It
   A. reveals to supervisors the degree to which ideas that are passed down are accepted by subordinates
   B. reduces the participation of subordinates in the operation of the department
   C. encourages subordinates to try for promotion
   D. enables supervisors to learn more readily what the *grapevine* is saying

16. A supervisor may be informed through either oral or written reports. Which one of the following is an ADVANTAGE of using oral reports? 16.____
    A. There is no need for a formal record of the report.
    B. An exact duplicate of the report is not easily transmitted to others.
    C. A good oral report requires little time for preparation.
    D. An oral report involves two-way communication between a subordinate and his supervisor.

17. Of the following, the MOST important reason why supervisors should communicate effectively with the public is to 17.____
    A. improve the public's understanding of information that is important for them to know
    B. establish a friendly relationship
    C. obtain information about the kinds of people who come to the agency
    D. convince the public that services are adequate

18. Supervisors should generally NOT use phrases like *too hard*, *too easy*, and *a lot* PRINCIPALLY because such phrases 18.____
    A. may be offensive to some minority groups
    B. are too informal
    C. mean different things to different people
    D. are difficult to remember

19. The ability to communicate clearly and concisely is an important element in effective leadership. 19.____
    Which of the following statements about oral and written communication is GENERALLY true?
    A. Oral communication is more time-consuming.
    B. Written communication is more likely to be misinterpreted.
    C. Oral communication is useful only in emergencies.
    D. Written communication is useful mainly when giving information to fewer than twenty people.

20. Rumors can often have harmful and disruptive effects on an organization. Which one of the following is the BEST way to prevent rumors from becoming a problem? 20.____
    A. Refuse to act on rumors, thereby making them less believable.
    B. Increase the amount of information passed along by the *grapevine*.
    C. Distribute as much factual information as possible.
    D. Provide training in report writing.

21. Suppose that a subordinate asks you about a rumor he has heard. The rumor deals with a subject which your superiors consider *confidential*. 21.____
    Which of the following BEST describes how you should answer the subordinate? Tell

A. the subordinate that you don't make the rules and that he should speak to higher ranking officials
B. the subordinate that you will ask your superior for information
C. him only that you cannot comment on the matter
D. him the rumor is not true

22. Supervisors often find it difficult to *get their message across* when instructing newly appointed employees in their various duties. 22.____
The MAIN reason for this is generally that the
A. duties of the employees have increased
B. supervisor is often so expert in his area that he fails to see it from the learner's point of view
C. supervisor adapts his instruction to the slowest learner in the group
D. new employees are younger, less concerned with job security and more interested in fringe benefits

23. Assume that you are discussing a job problem with an employee under your supervision. During the discussion, you see that the man's eyes are turning away from you and that he is not paying attention. 23.____
In order to get the man's attention, you should FIRST
A. ask him to look you in the eye
B. talk to him about sports
C. tell him he is being very rude
D. change your tone of voice

24. As a supervisor, you may find it necessary to conduct meetings with your subordinates. 24.____
Of the following, which would be MOST helpful in assuring that a meeting accomplishes the purpose for which it was called?
A. Give notice of the conclusions you would like to reach at the start of the meeting.
B. Delay the start of the meeting until everyone is present.
C. Write down points to be discussed in proper sequence.
D. Make sure everyone is clear on whatever conclusions have been reached and on what must be done after the meeting.

25. Every supervisor will occasionally be called upon to deliver a reprimand to a subordinate. If done properly, this can greatly help an employee improve his performance. 25.____
Which one of the following is NOT a good practice to follow when giving a reprimand?
A. Maintain your composure and temper
B. Reprimand a subordinate in the presence of other employees so they can learn the same lesson
C. Try to understand why the employee was not able to perform satisfactorily
D. Let your knowledge of the man involved determine the exact nature of the reprimand

KEY (CORRECT ANSWERS)

1.	C	11.	A
2.	B	12.	A
3.	D	13.	B
4.	B	14.	C
5.	D	15.	A
6.	C	16.	D
7.	C	17.	A
8.	B	18.	C
9.	C	19.	B
10.	C	20.	C

21. B
22. B
23. D
24. D
25. B

TEST 2

DIRECTIONS: Each question or incomplete statement is followed by several suggested answers or completions. Select the one that BEST answers the question or completes the statement. *PRINT THE LETTER OF THE CORRECT ANSWER IN THE SPACE AT THE RIGHT.*

1. Usually one thinks of communication as a single step, essentially that of transmitting an idea. 1.____
Actually, however, this is only part of a total process, the FIRST step of which should be
   A. the prompt dissemination of the idea to those who may be affected by it
   B. motivating those affected to take the required action
   C. clarifying the idea in one's own mind
   D. deciding to whom the idea is to be communicated

2. Research studies on patterns of informal communication have concluded that most individuals in a group tend to be passive recipients of news, while a few make it their business to spread it around in an organization. 2.____
With this conclusion in mind, it would be MOST correct for the supervisor to attempt to identify these few individuals and
   A. give them the complete facts on important matters in advance of others
   B. inform the other subordinates of the identity of these few individuals so that their influence may be minimized
   C. keep them straight on the facts on important matters
   D. warn them to cease passing along any information to others

3. The one of the following which is the PRINCIPAL advantage of making an oral report is that it 3.____
   A. affords an immediate opportunity for two-way communication between the subordinate and superior
   B. is an easy method for the superior to use in transmitting information to others of equal rank
   C. saves the time of all concerned
   D. permits more precise pinpointing of praise or blame by means of follow-up questions by the superior

4. An agency may sometimes undertake a public relations program of a defensive nature. 4.____
With reference to the use of defensive public relations, it would be MOST correct to state that it
   A. is bound to be ineffective since defensive statements, even though supported by factual data, can never hope to even partly overcome the effects of prior unfavorable attacks
   B. proves that the agency has failed to establish good relationships with newspapers, radio stations, or other means of publicity

C. shows that the upper echelons of the agency have failed to develop sound public relations procedures and techniques
D. is sometimes required to aid morale by protecting the agency from unjustified criticism and misunderstanding of policies or procedures

5. Of the following factors which contribute to possible undesirable public attitudes towards an agency, the one which is MOST susceptible to being changed by the efforts of the individual employee in an organization is that 5.____
A. enforcement of unpopular regulations as offended many individuals
B. the organization itself has an unsatisfactory reputation
C. the public is not interested in agency matters
D. there are many errors in judgment committed by individual subordinates

6. It is not enough for an agency's services to be of a high quality; attention must also be given to the acceptability of these services to the general public. 6.____
This statement is GENERALLY
A. *false*; a superior quality of service automatically wins public support
B. *true*; the agency cannot generally progress beyond the understanding and support of the public
C. *false*; the acceptance by the public of agency services determines their quality
D. *true*; the agency is generally unable to engage in any effective enforcement activity without public support

7. Sustained agency participation in a program sponsored by a community organization is MOST justified when 7.____
A. the achievement of agency objectives in some area depends partly on the activity of this organization
B. the community organization is attempting to widen the base of participation in all community affairs
C. the agency is uncertain as to what the community wants
D. the agency is uncertain as to what the community wants

8. Of the following, the LEAST likely way in which a records system may serve a supervisor is in 8.____
A. developing a sympathetic and cooperative public attitude toward the agency
B. improving the quality of supervision by permitting a check on the accomplishment of subordinates
C. permit a precise prediction of the exact incidences in specific categories for the following year
D. helping to take the guesswork out of the distribution of the agency

9. Assuming that the *grapevine* in any organization is virtually indestructible, the one of the following which it is MOST important for management to understand is: 9.____
   A. What is being spread by means of the *grapevine* and the reason for spreading it
   B. What is being spread by means of the *grapevine* and how it is being spread
   C. Who is involved in spreading the information that is on the *grapevine*
   D. Why those who are involved in spreading the information are doing so

10. When the supervisor writes a report concerning an investigation to which he has been assigned, it should be LEAST intended to provide 10.____
    A. a permanent official record of relevant information gathered
    B. a summary of case findings limited to facts which tend to indicate the guilt of a suspect
    C. a statement of the facts on which higher authorities may base a corrective or disciplinary action
    D. other investigators with information so that they may continue with other phases of the investigation

11. In survey work, questionnaires rather than interviews are sometimes used. The one of the following which is a DISADVANTAGE of the questionnaire method as compared with the interview is the 11.____
    A. difficulty of accurately interpreting the results
    B. problem of maintaining anonymity of the participant
    C. fact that it is relatively uneconomical
    D. requirement of special training for the distribution of questionnaires

12. in his contacts with the public, an employee should attempt to create a good climate of support for his agency. 12.____
    This statement is GENERALLY
    A. *false*; such attempts are clearly beyond the scope of his responsibility
    B. *true*; employees of an agency who come in contact with the public have the opportunity to affect public relations
    C. *false*; such activity should be restricted to supervisors trained in public relations techniques
    D. *true*; the future expansion of the agency depends to a great extent on continued public support of the agency

13. The repeated use by a supervisor of a call for volunteers to get a job done is objectionable MAINLY because it 13.____
    A. may create a feeling of animosity between the volunteers and the non-volunteers
    B. may indicate that the supervisor is avoiding responsibility for making assignments which will be most productive
    C. is an indication that the supervisor is not familiar with the individual capabilities of his men
    D. is unfair to men who, for valid reasons, do not, or cannot volunteer

14. Of the following statements concerning subordinates' expressions to a supervisor of their opinions and feelings concerning work situations, the one which is MOST correct is that 14.____
    A. by listening and responding to such expressions the supervisor encourages the development of complaints
    B. the lack of such expressions should indicate to the supervisor that there is a high level of job satisfaction
    C. the more the supervisor listens to and responds to such expressions, the more he demonstrates lack of supervisory ability
    D. by listening and responding to such expressions, the supervisor will enable many subordinates to understand and solve their own problems on the job

15. In attempting to motivate employees, rewards are considered preferable to punishment PRIMARILY because 15.____
    A. punishment seldom has any effect on human behavior
    B. punishment usually results in decreased production
    C. supervisors find it difficult to punish
    D. rewards are more likely to result in willing cooperation

16. In an attempt to combat the low morale in his organization, a high level supervisor publicized an *open-door policy* to allow employees who wished to do so to come to him with their complaints. 16.____
    Which of the following is LEAST likely to account for the fact that no employee came in with a complaint?
    A. Employees are generally reluctant to go over the heads of their immediate supervisor.
    B. The employees did not feel that management would help them.
    C. The low morale was not due to complaints associated with the job.
    D. The employees felt that they had more to lose than to gain.

17. It is MOST desirable to use written instructions rather than oral instructions for a particular job when 17.____
    A. a mistake on the job will not be serious
    B. the job can be completed in a short time
    C. there is no need to explain the job minutely
    D. the job involves many details

18. If you receive a telephone call regarding a matter which your office does not handle, you should FIRST 18.____
    A. give the caller the telephone number of the proper office so that he can dial again
    B. offer to transfer the caller to the proper office
    C. suggest that the caller re-dial since he probably dialed incorrectly
    D. tell the caller he has reached the wrong office and then hang up

19. When you answer the telephone, the MOST important reason for identifying yourself and your organization is to 19.____
   A. give the caller time to collect his or her thoughts
   B. impress the caller with your courtesy
   C. inform the caller that he or she has reached the right number
   D. set a business-like tone at the beginning of the conversation

20. As soon as you pick up the phone, a very angry caller begins immediately to complain about city agencies and *red tape*. He says that he has been shifted to two or three different offices. It turs out that he is seeking information which is not immediately available to you. You believe, you know, however, where it can be found. 20.____
Which of the following actions is the BEST one for you to take?
   A. To eliminate all confusion, suggest that the caller write the agency stating explicitly what he wants.
   B. Apologize by telling the caller how busy city agencies now are, but also tell him directly that you do not have the information he needs.
   C. Ask for the caller's telephone number and assure him you will call back after you have checked further.
   D. Give the caller the name and telephone number of the person who might be able to help, but explain that you are not positive he will get results/

21. Which of the following approaches usually provides the BEST communication in the objectives and values of a new program which is to be introduced? 21.____
   A. A general written description of the program by the program manager for review by those who share responsibility
   B. An effective verbal presentation by the program manager to those affected
   C. Development of the plan and operational approach in carrying out the program by the program manager assisted by his key subordinates
   D. Development of the plan by the program manager's supervisor

22. What is the BEST approach for introducing change? 22.____
A
   A. combination of written and also verbal communication to all personnel affected by the change
   B. general bulletin to all personnel
   C. meeting pointing out all the values of the new approach
   D. written directive to key personnel

23. Of the following, committees are BEST used for 23.____
   A. advising the head of the organization
   B. improving functional work
   C. making executive decisions
   D. making specific planning decisions

24. An effective discussion leader is one who 24.____
    A. announces the problem and his preconceived solution at the start of the discussion
    B. guides and directs the discussion according to pre-arranged outline
    C. interrupts or corrects confused participants to save time
    D. permits anyone to say anything at any time

25. The human relations movement in management theory is basically concerned with 25.____
    A. counteracting employee unrest
    B. eliminating the *time and motion* man
    C. interrelationships among individuals in organizations
    D. the psychology of the worker

KEY (CORRECT ANSWERS)

1. C
2. C
3. A
4. D
5. D

6. B
7. A
8. C
9. A
10. B

11. A
12. B
13. B
14. D
15. D

16. C
17. D
18. B
19. C
20. C

21. C
22. A
23. A
24. B
25. C

EXAMINATION SECTION

TEST 1

DIRECTIONS: Each question or incomplete statement is followed by several suggested answers or completions. Select the one that BEST answers the question or completes the statement. *PRINT THE LETTER OF THE CORRECT ANSWER IN THE SPACE AT THE RIGHT.*

1. A group member who starts out at the same level as other group members and is able to move into a leadership position within that group would be described as what kind of a leader? 1.____
   A. Autocratic B. Democratic C. Emergent D. Informal

2. Your boss is only effective as the leader of your department when you and your coworkers are motivated experts on the topic at hand. If any of you do not really have expertise in a given field, his leadership falters somewhat. What type of leader is your boss? 2.____
   A. Laissez-faire B. Technical C. Democratic D. Autocratic

3. If a leader is in charge of an inexperienced group that does not have the appropriate information and proficiency to successfully complete a task, which of the following approaches should the leader use in order for success to follow within the group? 3.____
   A. Yelling B. Delegating C. Participating D. Selling

4. If you are a democratic leader, which of the following styles will be reflective of your leadership technique? 4.____
   A. Participating B. Telling C. Yelling D. Delegating

5. In producing equality in group member participation, which of the following should a leader NOT do? 5.____
   A. Make a statement or ask a question after each person in the group has said something
   B. Avoid taking a position during disagreements
   C. Limit comments to specific individuals within the group
   D. Control dominating speakers

6. Social capital is BEST defined as 6.____
   A. social connections that help us make more money
   B. social connections that improve our lives
   C. a type of connection that experts believe is becoming more common in Europe than the United States.
   D. none of the above

7. Communication is not simply sending a message. It is creating true 7.____
   A. connectivity B. understanding
   C. empathy D. power

8. Of the following, which is NOT a part of the speech communication process? 8.____
   A. Feedback B. Central idea
   C. Interference D. Ethics

9. You are leading a meeting and afterwards your colleagues tell you they didn't quite understand what you were communicating verbally and nonverbally to them. Which part of the communication process do you need to work on? 9.____
   A. Channel B. Main idea
   C. Message D. Specific purpose

10. If nonverbal messages contradict verbal symbols, you are sending what kind of message to your public? 10.____
   A. Clear B. Mixed
   C. Controversial D. Negative

11. Which of the following would a public speaker use to deliver verbal symbols? 11.____
   A. Words B. Gestures
   C. Tone D. Facial expression

12. You are in the process of taking a course on interacting with the public. Your instructor starts talking about "the pathway" used to transmit a message. He explains that "the pathway" is better known as a 12.____
   A. link B. loop C. transmitter D. channel

13. You finish an informational meeting with members of a community concerning a new park that will be built nearby. Afterwards, you are seeking feedback from them. Which of the following would NOT be a form of helpful feedback to you? 13.____
   A. Listeners raise their hands to point out a mistake
   B. Videotape the presentation
   C. Have colleagues and/or friends critique your presentation
   D. Hand out evaluation forms to listeners and have them fill it out after the presentation

14. Many public speaking experts have often repeated the famous quote, "A yawn is a silent _____," which references the quality of engagement within a presentation. 14.____
   A. rudeness B. insult C. shout D. protest

15. If a child is running around during your speech and making a lot of noise, what type of interference would that be? 15.____
   A. Situational B. External C. Internal D. Intentional

16. According to multiple recent surveys, of the five biggest mistakes that speakers make during a presentation, which one is the WORST? 16.____
   A. Being poorly prepared
   B. Trying to cover too much in one speech
   C. Failing to tailor a speech to the needs and interests of the audience
   D. Being boring

17. One of your colleagues has been asked to lead a meeting, and she confides in you that she suffers from excessive stage fright. Which of the following areas should you advise her to focus on to prevent her fear? 17.____
   A. Preparation
   B. Self-confidence
   C. Experience
   D. Sense of humor

18. When interacting with the public, which of the following elements should you NEVER imagine before engaging in public speaking? 18.____
   A. Effective delivery
   B. Nervousness
   C. Possibility of failure
   D. Success

19. A spokesperson is giving a speech to community members and you are evaluating him. You notice he tends to focus too much on himself and not enough on his audience. What is one piece of advice you can give him so he can shift his focus more to his audience? 19.____
   A. Change his amount of eye contact
   B. Work on facial expressions
   C. Alter his style of speaking
   D. All of the above

20. Most experts agree that the best way to eliminate excess energy would be to do all of the following EXCEPT 20.____
   A. using visual aids
   B. gripping the lectern
   C. walking to the right and left occasionally
   D. making gestures

21. A woman has lived in Newville her whole life. Recently, the Newville public works department made a policy change that angered her since it completely rearranged her schedule. She calls you on the phone and displays her displeasure with your department's recent policy change. What is the FIRST response you should have toward her? 21.____
   A. Interrupt her to say you cannot discuss the situation until she calms down
   B. Apologize to her that she has been negatively affected by the public works department
   C. Listen to her and demonstrate comprehension of her situation and why she was upset by your department's action
   D. Give her a detailed explanation of the reasons for the policy change

22. Which of the following is generally TRUE regarding public opinion? 22.____
   A. It is hard to move people toward a strong opinion on anything
   B. It is easy to move people toward a strong opinion on anything
   C. Most public relations are devoted to repairing negative public opinion about individuals
   D. It is easier than previously thought to move people away from an opinion they hold

23. Influencing a community member's attitude really comes down to which of the following? 23.____
   A. Journalism
   B. Public relations
   C. Social psychology
   D. Social action groups

24. If you attend a town hall meeting in which community members will bring up issues that require you to explain why your organization made the decisions it made, you will need to persuade them using evidence that is virtually indisputable. Which type of evidence should you stick to when explaining answers to the public? 24.____
    A. Facts
    B. Personal experience
    C. Emotions
    D. Using what appeals to the target public

25. In the last decade, especially after all the organizational and governmental scandals, public institutions must do which of the following in order to be successful? 25.____
    A. Work hard to earn and sustain favorable public opinion
    B. Trust the instincts expressed by the general public
    C. Be cognizant of the media's power
    D. Place the needs of the executives ahead of the needs of the public and other constituents

KEY (CORRECT ANSWERS)

1.	C	11.	A
2.	A	12.	D
3.	B	13.	A
4.	D	14.	C
5.	A	15.	B
6.	B	16.	C
7.	B	17.	A
8.	D	18.	B
9.	C	19.	D
10.	B	20.	B

21.	C
22.	D
23.	B
24.	A
25.	A

TEST 2

DIRECTIONS: Each question or incomplete statement is followed by several suggested answers or completions. Select the one that BEST answers the question or completes the statement. *PRINT THE LETTER OF THE CORRECT ANSWER IN THE SPACE AT THE RIGHT.*

1. Unique attributes of the Internet that people can enjoy include all of the following EXCEPT 1.____
   A. immediacy
   B. low cost
   C. pervasiveness
   D. value for building one-to-one human relationships

2. Which of the following is a reason that social media can be more effective than traditional means of advertising and communication? 2.____
   A. When someone mentions your brand in social media, there is much more potential for other people to notice
   B. It is easier to decipher tone and purpose through Twitter or Facebook than through personal communication
   C. Most of the people who would be interested in your brand or service are comfortable and familiar with using social media
   D. Almost anyone can step into a media relations role if primarily using social media, because it is easy to communicate effectively through social media platforms

3. You are tasked with building publicity for the upcoming reveal of a new art installation in the town you work in. Your boss tells you to contact journalists, reporters and bloggers to help spread the word. Which of the following would be the MOST effective way of getting the media to help build coverage? 3.____
   A. Send out a mass e-mail to any media members in the area detailing the art installation and why you need coverage for it
   B. Call each media outlet and find out who would most likely cover and build publicity for your project. Then reach out to them either face-to-face or through a phone call
   C. Using Twitter, tweet at the media members and introduce yourself and your art installation and ask them to help spread the word
   D. None of the above

4. When using written communication, which of the following is a MAJOR challenge of writing to listeners? 4.____
   A. Providing lots of statistics
   B. Grabbing the attention of the listener quickly
   C. Providing information that is easily reviewed
   D. Presenting lots of incidentals

5. In order to communicate well in writing, which of the following pieces of advice sounds good but doesn't actually help you? 5.____
   A. Write material for all audiences rather than focusing on one
   B. Think before writing
   C. Write simply and with clarity
   D. Write and rewrite until you have a polished, finished product

6. You send out a public newsletter that details a project that your team is currently working on. One week later, an employee on your team tells you she has received multiple phone calls from confused constituents claiming that the newsletter's readability was low. When you send out a corrected newsletter, you need to make sure that your communication is easy to 6.____
   A. read B. hear C. edit D. comprehend

7. You work for a biomedical company as a public outreach advocate. One day, an exciting e-mail circulates internally that states one of your scientists has discovered a cure for leukemia and your supervisor tasks you with writing the release. When writing the release, the newsworthy element inherent in the story is 7.____
   A. oddity B. conflict C. impact D. proximity

8. When communicating with the public through the Internet, news releases 8.____
   A. should not be sent via e-mail B. should be succinct
   C. should be sent via "snail mail" D. none of the above

9. What is the MAJOR advantage of organizational publications? Their ability to 9.____
   A. give sponsoring organizations a means of uncontrolled communications
   B. deliver specific, detailed information to narrowly defined target publics
   C. avoid the problems typically associated with two-way media
   D. provide a revenue source for sponsoring organizations

10. You are confronted by a question from a reporter that you do not know the answer to. What should you do? 10.____
    A. Give them other information you are certain is right
    B. Tell them that information is "off the record" and will be distributed later
    C. Say "no comment" rather than look like you're uninformed
    D. Admit that you don't know but promise to provide the information later

11. Often times, an organization will run situation analysis before they share information with the public. Which one of these "internal factors" is usually associated with a situational analysis? 11.____
    A. A communication audit B. Community focus groups
    C. A list of media contacts D. Strategy suggestions

12. When you are hired, your first task is to start a process of identifying who are involved and affected by a situation central to your organization. This process is MOST commonly referred to as a(n) 12.____
    A. situation interview
    B. communication audit
    C. exploratory survey
    D. stakeholder analysis

13. Once a public outreach plan is in the summative evaluation phase, which of the following is generally associated with it? 13.____
    A. Impact
    B. Implementation
    C. Attitude change
    D. Preparation

14. Which of the following Internet-related challenges is MOST significant in the public relations field? 14.____
    A. Finding stable, cost-effective internet provides
    B. Representing clients using new social media environments
    C. Staying abreast of changing technology
    D. Training staff to use social media

15. Which of the following BEST defines a public issue? Any 15.____
    A. problem that brings a public lawsuit
    B. concern that is of mutual distress to competitors
    C. issue that is of mutual concern to an organization and its stakeholders
    D. problem that is not a concern to an organization and/or one of its stakeholders

16. A handful of people are posting misleading and/or negative information about your organization. What is the MOST proactive approach to handling this situation? 16.____
    A. Buy up enough shares in the site where the negative posts are, and prevent those users from posting again
    B. Post anonymous comments on the sites to help combat the negativity
    C. Prepare news releases that discredit the inaccuracies
    D. Make policy changes to address complaints highlighted on the sites

17. Your supervisor has recently asked you to review present and future realities for interacting with the public. Why is it important to continually review these? 17.____
    A. It helps develop your vision statement
    B. It helps interpret trends for management
    C. It helps construe the organization's business plan
    D. To know what path the company should pursue

18. You are the community relations director for the public water utility plant that has been the focus of a group of activists who are opposed to the addition of fluoride to drinking water. These objectors are not only at the plant each day, but they are also very active on social media inciting negativity towards the practice. As the director of the plant, you have overwhelming evidence that contradicts what the protestors are arguing. You want to combat their social media with your own internet plan. Which of the following is the MOST appropriate action for you to take? 18.____
    A. Use utility employees to write the blog, posing as healthcare professionals
    B. Reach out to medical professionals to volunteer to tweet and message community members under their own identities, but with no reference to the utility company
    C. Write a blog yourself, identifying yourself as an employee, and quote the scientific opinions of a variety of sources
    D. Pay for medical professionals to respond through the internet, identifying the utility as their sponsor, but without disclosing the compensation

19. You have recently completed an advertising campaign to help assuage the anger of the community at changes in the upcoming summer program for the city. Which of the following measurements would be MOST effective for evaluating the campaign's impact on audience attitude? 19.____
    A. A content analysis of media coverage
    B. Studying blog postings about the issue
    C. Analyzing pre- and post-numbers of people signed up for the summer programs
    D. Conducting a pre- and post-analysis of public opinions

20. In order to measure how policy changes will affect the public, you recommend that your supervisors first run a focus group for research. They like the idea, but want you to be in charge of running the group. Which of the following should you keep in mind as you form the focus group? 20.____
    A. Participants need to be randomly selected
    B. Make sure participants are radically different from one another so you get a range of opinions
    C. Include at least seven or more people in the group. Otherwise, the sample is too small to draw any conclusions.
    D. Formulate a research plan and use it as a script so you can make sure the results are ones that will work for you and your supervisors

21. The public university has recently come under fire for not offering enough tuition savings options for students. You have been hired to help promote the programs they offer including new savings programs. What is the MOST appropriate first step for you to take? 21.____
    A. Research pricing and development costs for the services
    B. Develop a survey to discover which factors impact families' savings
    C. Conduct a situation analysis to gain better understanding of the issues
    D. Hold a focus group to determine which messages would be most effective for your program

22. After receiving feedback from the public on a new program, you are concerned the results have been tainted by courtesy bias. You plan on sending out a new questionnaire, but you need to make sure the bias is discouraged in it. Which of the following techniques will be MOST effective at decreasing the partiality? 22.____
    A. Make questionnaire responses confidential
    B. Employ an outside firm to run the survey
    C. Offer a larger range of responses in the survey
    D. Both "A" and "C"

23. You have just relocated from Omaha, Nebraska to a branch in Chicago, Illinois. In order to communicate well while in Chicago, you must remember that 23.____
    A. most publics have the same needs
    B. all publics are most interested only in technology you are using
    C. each audience has its own special needs and require different types of communication
    D. all audiences' needs overlap

24. Recently, the Parks and Recreation Department has come under fire because it has been accused of too much marketing and not enough public relations. Which of the following, if true, would lend credibility to these accusations? 24.____
    A. Employees are focused on signing citizens up for as many different camps and activities available over the summer as possible
    B. Management consistently tries to send appreciation gifts to members of the community when they have volunteered or attending an activity sponsored by the Park district
    C. Weekly meetings are held to determine how to best improve the Park district's image as it relates to consumers
    D. Parks and Recreation is primarily focused on making sure the public enjoys their activities and trusts them to put on educational programs for the children

25. During your speech, a community member stands up and accuses you of "spinning" a story. Which of the following BEST describes their accusation? 25.____
    A. You are relating a message through an agreed-upon ethical practice within the public relations community
    B. You are twisting a message to create performance where there is none
    C. You are trying to preserve hard-earned credibility
    D. You are providing the media with balanced and accurate information

KEY (CORRECT ANSWERS)

1. D
2. A
3. C
4. B
5. D
6. D
7. C
8. B
9. B
10. D
11. A
12. D
13. A
14. C
15. C
16. B
17. A
18. C
19. D
20. A
21. C
22. D
23. C
24. A
25. B

TEST 3

DIRECTIONS: Each question or incomplete statement is followed by several suggested answers or completions. Select the one that BEST answers the question or completes the statement. *PRINT THE LETTER OF THE CORRECT ANSWER IN THE SPACE AT THE RIGHT.*

1. In order to be successful in relating to the public, all of the following are vital EXCEPT 1.____
   A. performance
   B. relationship building
   C. formal education
   D. diversity of experience

2. Which of the following is TRUE of communicating well regarding public relations experts? 2.____
   A. It will differentiate you and your role from others with special skills in the organization you work for
   B. It should be handled delicately in order to avoid upsetting stakeholders
   C. It is not as important as looking fashionable
   D. It is less important than understanding bureaucratic peculiarities

3. You are critiquing a staffer who will lead an important meeting in two days and you note that she keeps using words that are steeped with connotation. You tell her to be careful of these words. Why? 3.____
   A. They transmit meaning too clearly, and you always want to leave wiggle room in your meaning
   B. They transmit the dictionary definition of a word that makes for a boring presentation
   C. They transmit meaning with an emotional overtone that could lead to misunderstanding in an overall message
   D. They lend themselves to stereotyping

4. If you are trying to avoid biasing your intended audience, which of the following factors could help with that? 4.____
   A. Symbols
   B. Objective reporting by media
   C. Semantics
   D. Peers

5. Of the following, which trait is MOST desirable when working with the public? 5.____
   A. Having the "gift for gab"
   B. Being an elite strategist
   C. Being able to leap organizational boundaries
   D. Performing well, especially in crises

6. Which of the following areas is likely to see continual growth in the practice of public relations? 6.____
   A. Healthcare
   B. Social media
   C. Law enforcement
   D. None of the above

7. What is the MOST commonly used public relations tactic? 7.____
   A. A news release
   B. A special event
   C. A PSA (public service announcement)
   D. A full feature news article

8. You have just been assigned to help with a new advertising campaign that will promote the new services offered by your organization. One major component of the new campaign will focus on publicity through photographs. Knowing you need to get this part of the project right, which of the following is the BEST tip to remember when taking PR photos? 8.____
   A. Don't use action shots because they usually wind up blurry
   B. Make sure there is good contrast and sharp detail
   C. Ensure that the product/services are the biggest thing(s) in the photo
   D. Photograph multiple people rather than only one

9. Which of the following situations would merit holding a press conference? 9.____
   A. When a corporation is restructured
   B. When a new public relations employee has been hired
   C. When information is of minor relevance to a specific audience
   D. When there is a new product to be released

10. On average, how long should an announcement to the public last on the radio? 10.____
    A. 2 minutes B. 20 seconds C. 1 minute D. 10 seconds

11. In educating the public, you need to develop a PR plan and analyze each situation that could arise. Which of the following should NOT be a part of the analysis? 11.____
    A. Research B. Message crafting
    C. Creating a problem statement D. Asking the 5 W's and the H

12. You are in charge of promoting an event in the near future, but social media is unavailable to you at this time. Which of the following is the BEST way to get your message out to the media and, therefore, the public? 12.____
    A. An Op-Ed piece in the local newspaper
    B. A press conference
    C. A newsletter
    D. A news release

13. In the past few months, you and your colleagues have been accused of "doublespeak". Which of the following excerpts from presentations you have used could you defend and explain why it would NOT be an example of "doublespeak"? 13.____
    A. You called combat "fighting"
    B. Fred referred to genocide as "ethnic cleansing"
    C. Your boss referred to recent layoffs as "downsizing"
    D. Susie called the janitor a "custodial engineer"

14. In relating to the public, which of the following reflects key words in defining modern day PR? 14.____
    A. Deliberate, public interest, management function
    B. Persuasive, manipulative, improvisation
    C. Management, technical, flexible
    D. Influential, creative, evaluative

15. How is educating and relating to the public different from being a journalist, marketing agent, or advertiser? 15.____
    A. It is more focused on advocacy
    B. It is about getting "free" press coverage
    C. It is about building relationships with various demographics
    D. All of the above

16. Of the following, what is the BEST tactic for learning employee attitudes? 16.____
    A. Internal communications audit
    B. Research
    C. Conference meeting
    D. Both A and B

17. When releasing news to the public, you should make sure it reads at a _____-grade reading level. 17.____
    A. 5th
    B. 12th
    C. 9th
    D. 7th

18. If you are using a euphemism that actually changes the meaning/impact of a concept you are trying to relay, what is that called? 18.____
    A. Insider language
    B. Doublespeak
    C. Stylizing
    D. Plagiarism

19. Which of the following should be included in a public relations campaign if you want to ensure people will hear, understand, and believe your message? 19.____
    A. Repetition
    B. Imagery
    C. Thoroughness
    D. Acceptance

20. In PR, what is it called when you track coverage and compare it over a period of time? 20.____
    A. Bookmarking
    B. Benchmarking
    C. Comparison analysis
    D. Correspondence

21. What is a baseline study PRIMARILY used for? 21.____
    A. To determine changes in audience perception and attitude
    B. To figure out how well your company is doing in the marketplace compared to your competitors
    C. To find out the cost of buying space taken up by a particular article if that article is an advertisement
    D. None of the above

22. Of the following people, who would BEST be considered a modern role model for successful public relations? 22.____
    A. Phineas T. Barnum (Barnum and Bailey)
    B. Ivy Lee
    C. Andrew Jackson
    D. Sir Walter Raleigh

23. If your organization has recently participated in a "publicity stunt," what type of PR strategy have you just used? 23.____
    A. Community
    B. Lobbying
    C. News management
    D. Crisis management

24. You tell your supervisor that you want to start using video press releases. When he presses you to explain why, you tell him that you want to take advantage of the fact that 24.____
    A. many news agencies don't review them ahead of broadcasting
    B. most reporters hired to create them have contacts within the industry
    C. they cover stories that some local news organizations cannot
    D. the production value may be better than those at local stations

25. A _____ is a type of news leak in which the source reveals large policy changes are on the table. 25.____
    A. disclosure
    B. hook
    C. exclusive
    D. trial balloon

KEY (CORRECT ANSWERS)

1.	C	11.	B
2.	B	12.	D
3.	C	13.	A
4.	B	14.	A
5.	D	15.	D
6.	B	16.	D
7.	A	17.	C
8.	B	18.	B
9.	D	19.	A
10.	C	20.	B

21.	A
22.	B
23.	C
24.	C
25.	D

TEST 4

DIRECTIONS: Each question or incomplete statement is followed by several suggested answers or completions. Select the one that BEST answers the question or completes the statement. *PRINT THE LETTER OF THE CORRECT ANSWER IN THE SPACE AT THE RIGHT.*

1. The Facial Feedback Hypothesis is a popular nonverbal theory that is BEST defined as 1.____
   A. people mirroring each other's facial expressions
   B. emotions leading to certain facial expressions
   C. facial expression can lead to the experience of certain emotions
   D. looking into a mirror while making a facial expression can cause one to change their facial expression

2. Of the following, which is NOT recognized as a function of smiling? 2.____
   A. It provides feedback.
   B. It signals disinterest.
   C. It helps establish rapport.
   D. It signals attentiveness.

3. When facial expressions are limited by cultural expectations, that is referred to as 3.____
   A. display rules
   B. syntactic displays
   C. adaptors
   D. interaction intensification

4. Of the following, which is recognized as part of the six basic emotions across cultures globally? 4.____
   A. Guilt
   B. Happiness
   C. Fear
   D. Both B and C

5. Which kinds of communication scenarios are more likely to see leadership roles develop from? 5.____
   A. Small group
   B. Intrapersonal communication
   C. Face-to-face public communication
   D. Text messaging

6. Which of the following highlights the key difference between small group communication and organizational communication? 6.____
   A. Feedback is easier and more immediate in organizational.
   B. Communication is more informal in small group communication.
   C. The message is easier to adapt to the specific needs of the receiver in organizational communication.
   D. People are more spread out in small group communication.

7. Which of the following would be an example of mediated communication? 7.____
   A. A principal addresses the student body in a speech.
   B. Two friends communicate while they work together in class.
   C. An employee texts his coworkers to see if they want to hang out after work.
   D. Three friends joke with one another while attending a concert.

8. Which of the following is FALSE concerning the way interpersonal relationships can affect us physically? 8.____
   A. Without interpersonal relationships, we can become sick
   B. These interpersonal relationships are necessary for humans; according to most research, humans raised in isolation are less healthy than those raised with others
   C. Humans are not the only mammals that need relationships in order to survive and thrive
   D. Interpersonal relationships are necessary until about age 12, but not later in adulthood

9. Which of the following is a characteristic of public relationships as they compare to private relationships? 9.____
   A. Intrinsic rewards
   B. Normative rules
   C. Use of particularistic knowledge
   D. Small number of intimates

10. When someone asks how you know they were angry, it is likely they fall into which style of facial expressions? 10.____
   A. Withholder
   B. Revealer
   C. Frozen-affect expressor
   D. Unwitting expressor

11. The theory of expectancy violations is BEST defined as 11.____
   A. nonverbal behavior reciprocated based primarily on positive or negative valence and the perceived reward value of the other person
   B. the process of intimacy exchange within a dyad relationship
   C. a social rule that says we should repay in kind what another has provided us
   D. none of the above

12. If an employee has a very good idea of what is and is not socially acceptable in any given situation, which kind of linguistic competence is she strong in? 12.____
   A. Phonemic
   B. Syntactic
   C. Pragmatic
   D. Semantic

13. Which of the following would NOT be considered sexist language? 13.____
   A. Although a girl, Sonia is very brave.
   B. A gorgeous model, Johnny also likes to use his surfboard on the weekends.
   C. Jimmy's brother is a male nurse.
   D. None; all are considered to be sexist.

14. What is it called when individual experience, and NOT conventional agreement, creates meaning? 14.____
   A. Small talk communication
   B. Denotative meaning
   C. Connotative meaning
   D. Self-reflexive communication

15. Which of the following kinds of communication do students spend the MOST time engaged in? 15.____
   A. Listening
   B. Writing
   C. Reading
   D. Speaking

16. Which of the following would be evidence of active listening? 16.____
    A. Maintain eye contact
    B. Nodding and making eye contact
    C. Asking for clarification
    D. All of the above

17. When listening in an evaluative context, which of the following must be done for it to be considered successful? 17.____
    A. Precisely disseminate stimuli in a message
    B. Comprehend the intended meaning of a message
    C. Make critical assessments of the accuracy of the facts in a message
    D. All of the above

18. A friend visits one day and tells you she thinks her husband is cheating on her with his ex-wife. She tells you she doesn't know what to do because she can't imagine living without him. If you wanted to paraphrase, which of the following BEST exemplifies that? 18.____
    A. "You are feeling insecure because you don't have a very good relationship with your husband."
    B. "You're afraid your husband is seeing his ex-wife behind your back; you don't know what to do; and you can't live without him."
    C. "You're afraid that your husband may still have feelings for his ex-wife and you're afraid you'll lose him."
    D. "Don't worry; his ex-wife is not back with him. You're just being paranoid."

19. When we form impressions of others, when might the recency effect impact our assessments? If we 19.____
    A. focus on our own feelings instead of the feelings of others
    B. are motivated to be more accurate or expect to be held accountable for our own perceptions
    C. engage in self-monitoring of our behaviors
    D. employ the discounting rule

20. Which of the following BEST defines a "modal self"? 20.____
    A. The ideal person for a social order
    B. A person who does not go to extremes
    C. The kind of self valued in the 20th century but not the 21st century
    D. The person who monitors his own behavior in social situations

21. Which of the following is TRUE of today's society? 21.____
    A. People are less selfish than they have ever been.
    B. People spend most of their time trying to be a single, unitary self.
    C. People have many short-lived relationships leading to their notions of themselves changing easily.
    D. People try to be frugal, honorable, and self-sacrificing.

22. A man's childhood consisted of a dismissing attachment style. Which of the following behaviors will he MOST likely exhibit as an adult? 22.____
    A. Anxiousness and ambivalence
    B. Obsessive friendliness and dependence
    C. Autonomy and distance from others
    D. Rhetorical sensitivity

23. When practicing self-disclosure, which of the following is a good rule of thumb? 23.____
    A. Be sure to disclose more than your partner
    B. Reserve your most important disclosures for people you know well
    C. Ignore the style of disclosure; the only thing that is important is content
    D. All of the above

24. During your first meeting as project leader, you approach your group and inform them that John will serve as your assistant project leader. He will be responsible for chairing team meetings and establishing the agenda. When John is given this formal leadership position, what type of power does he have over the other members of the project? 24.____
    A. Legitimate B. Reward C. Expert D. Punishment

25. If you bring an employee to lead a project because she is knowledgeable and skilled in the area the project focuses on, what type of power does she possess? 25.____
    A. Legitimate B. Reward C. Referent D. Expert

KEY (CORRECT ANSWERS)

1.	C	11.	A
2.	B	12.	C
3.	A	13.	D
4.	D	14.	C
5.	A	15.	A
6.	B	16.	D
7.	C	17.	C
8.	D	18.	B
9.	B	19.	D
10.	D	20.	A

21.	C
22.	C
23.	B
24.	A
25.	D

EXAMINATION SECTION

TEST 1

DIRECTIONS: Each question or incomplete statement is followed by several suggested answers or completions. Select the one that BEST answers the question or completes the statement. *PRINT THE LETTER OF THE CORRECT ANSWER IN THE SPACE AT THE RIGHT.*

1. A specialist is meeting with a panel of local community leaders to determine their perceptions about the effectiveness of a recent outreach program. The leaders seem unresponsive to the specialist's questions, looking at the floor or each other without directly answering the specialist's questions. 1.____
One strategy that might work to elicit the desired information would be to
   A. try to discern the hidden meaning of their silence
   B. adopt a mildly confrontational tone and remind them of what's at stake in the community
   C. keep asking open-ended questions and wait patiently for responses
   D. tell them to come back when they're ready to tell you their opinions

2. Each of the following statements about maintaining a community's attention is true, EXCEPT: 2.____
   A. The more challenging it is to pay attention to a message, the more likely it is that it will be attended to
   B. Listeners will be more motivated to pay attention if a speech is personally meaningful
   C. People will be more likely to attend if a speaker pauses to suggest natural transitions in a speech
   D. Listeners will attend to messages that stand out

3. Each of the following is a key strategy to integrative bargaining among community members in conflict, EXCEPT 3.____
   A. focusing on positions, rather than interests
   B. separating the people from the problem
   C. aiming for an outcome based on an objectively identified standard
   D. using active listening skills, such as rephrasing and questioning

4. Which of the following is NOT one of the major variables to take into account when considering a community needs assessment? 4.____
   A. State of program development
   B. Resources available
   C. Demographics
   D. Community attitudes

5. Which of the following groups would probably be formed specifically for, or be involved in, the purpose of addressing a specific unmet community need? 5.____
   A. An existing consumer group
   B. A council of community representatives
   C. A committee
   D. An existing community organization

6. If a public outreach campaign designed to mobilize a community fails, the MOST likely reason for this failure is that the campaign 6.____
   A. was not specific about what it wanted people to do
   B. was overly serious and did not appeal to people's sense of humor
   C. offered no incentive for the audience to make a change
   D. did not use language that appealed to the audience's emotions

7. Nationwide, the rate of involvement of elderly people in community-based programs demonstrates that they are 7.____
   A. under-served when compared to other age groups
   B. served at about the same rate as other age groups
   C. over-served when compared to other age groups
   D. hardly served at all

8. In projecting the likelihood of an education program's success, a domestic violence specialist identifies every single event that must occur to complete the project. The specialist then arranges these events in sequential order and allocates time requirements for each. Finally, the total time is calculated and a model showing all their events and timelines is charted. 8.____
   The specialist has used
   A. a PERT chart
   B. a simulation
   C. a Markov model
   D. the critical path method

9. When working with members of a predominantly African-American community, specialists from other cultural backgrounds should be aware that African-Americans tend to express thoughts and feelings through descriptions of 9.____
   A. physically tangible sensations
   B. problems to be analyzed
   C. corresponding analogies
   D. spiritual issues

10. Local nonprofessionals should be considered useful to a specialist who is looking to undertake a community outreach or educational initiative. 10.____
    Which of the following is LEAST likely to be a characteristic or role demonstrated by these community members?
    A. Undertaking support functions at the agency
    B. Serving as a communication channel between the agency and clients
    C. Encouraging greater agency acceptance and credibility within the community
    D. Helping the agency to accomplish meaningful change

11. In working with Native American groups or clients, it is important to recognize that the GREATEST health problem facing their communities today is 11.____
    A. domestic violence
    B. depression and suicide
    C. alcoholism
    D. tuberculosis

12. A specialist is facilitating a cooperative conflict resolution session between community members who have different opinions about what kinds of intervention services should be offered by the local adult protective services agency. 12.____
Which of the following is NOT a guideline that should be followed in this process?
   A. Early in the negotiations, ask each party to name the issues on which they will positively not yield.
   B. Try to get the parties to view the issue from other points of view, beside the two or three conflicting ones.
   C. Have each side volunteer what it would be willing to do to resolve the conflict.
   D. At the end of the session, draw up a formal agreement with agreed-upon actions for both parties.

13. A specialist wants to evaluate the effectiveness of a local women's shelter. The shelter has suffered from lax participation, given the number of women who have been abused in the surrounding area. The specialist wants to speak with the women in the community who did not follow up on referrals to the shelter, and begins by visiting some of these women. After gaining the trust of these women, the specialist asks for the names of women they know who might be in need of help with a domestic violence situation. 13.____
The specialist's approach in this case is _____ sampling.
   A. maximum variation
   B. snowball
   C. convenience
   D. typical case

14. When it comes to perceiving messages, people typically DON'T 14.____
   A. tend to simplify causal connections and sometimes even seek a single cause to explain what may be a highly complex effect
   B. tend to perceive messages independently of a categorical framework, especially if the message may be distorted by such an interpretation
   C. have a predisposition toward accepting any pattern that a speaker offers to explain seemingly unconnected facts
   D. tend to interpret things in the way they are viewed by their reference group

15. The elder members of Native American communities, regardless of kinship, are MOST commonly referred to as 15.____
   A. the ancients
   B. father or mother
   C. grandfather or grandmother
   D. chiefs

16. Each of the following is typically an objective of community mobilization, EXCEPT: 16.____
   A. To convince existing community resources to alter their services or work together to address an unmet need
   B. To gather and distribute information to consumers and agencies about unmet needs

C. To publicize existing community resources and make them more accessible
D. To bring an unmet community need to public attention in order to achieve acceptance of and support for fulfilling the need

17. Research in community outreach shows that women often build friendships through shared positive feelings, whereas men often build friendships through — 17.____
A. metacommunication B. catharsis
C. impression management D. shared activities

18. Typically, the FIRST step in a community-needs assessment is to — 18.____
A. identify community's strengths
B. explore the nature of the neighborhood
C. get to know the area and its residents
D. talk to people in the community

19. Most public relations experts agree that _____ exposure(s) to a message is the minimum just to get the message noticed. If the aim of a public outreach campaign is action or a change in behavior, the agency budget must plan for more exposures. — 19.____
A. one B. two C. three D. four

20. In the program development/community liaison model of community work and public outreach, the PRIMARY constituency is considered to be — 20.____
A. community representatives and the service agency board or administrators
B. elected officials, social agencies, and interagency organizations
C. marginalized or oppressed population groups in a city or region
D. residents of a neighborhood, parish or rural county

21. Social or interpersonal problems in many African-American communities have their roots in — 21.____
A. personality deficits B. unresolved family conflicts
C. poor communication D. external stressors

22. A public outreach campaign should — 22.____
I. focus on short-term, measurable goals, rather than ultimate outcomes
II. try to alter entrenched attitudes within a short time, with powerfully worded messages
III. proceed in steps or phases, each of which lays out a mechanism that leads to the desired effect
IV. ignore causes that led to a problem, and instead focus on solutions

The CORRECT answer is:
A. I and II B. II and III C. III only D. I, II, III and IV

23. Research findings indicate that in listing preferences for helping professional attributes, individuals from culturally diverse groups are MOST likely to consider _____ as more important than _____. 23.____
   A. personality similarity; either race/ethnic similarity or attitude similarity
   B. therapist experience; any kind of similarity
   C. race/ethnic similarity; attitude similarity
   D. attitude similarity; race/ethnic similarity

24. Each of the following is considered to be an objective of community organization EXCEPT 24.____
   A. effecting changes in the distribution of decision-making power
   B. helping people develop and strengthen the traits of self-direction and cooperation
   C. effecting and maintaining the balance between needs and resources in a community
   D. helping people deal with their problems by developing alternative behaviors

25. A specialist is helping the adult protective services agency to design a public outreach campaign. The topic to be addressed is complex, public understanding is low, and most professionals at the agency feel that having more complete information might change the opinions of community members. Which method of pre-campaign research is probably MOST appropriate? 25.____
   A. Deliberative polling
   B. Attitude scales
   C. Surveys or questionnaires
   D. Focus groups

KEY (CORRECT ANSWERS)

1.	C	11.	C
2.	A	12.	A
3.	A	13.	B
4.	C	14.	B
5.	C	15.	C
6.	A	16.	B
7.	A	17.	D
8.	D	18.	B
9.	C	19.	C
10.	A	20.	A

21.	D
22.	C
23.	D
24.	D
25.	A

TEST 2

DIRECTIONS: Each question or incomplete statement is followed by several suggested answers or completions. Select the one that BEST answers the question or completes the statement. *PRINT THE LETTER OF THE CORRECT ANSWER IN THE SPACE AT THE RIGHT.*

1. A specialist has been called in to resolve a dispute between two community leaders who have been arguing about the level of service needed within the community. The discussion has been going on for several hours when the specialist arrives, and both people seem to be upset. 1.____
After calming the two down and getting each of them to agree on a statement of the problem, the specialist should ask each person to
   A. summarize his or her argument in three main points
   B. explain why he or she became so upset
   C. clearly state, in objective terms, the position of the other in a form that meets with the other's approval
   D. identify the best alternative outcome, other than their presumed ideal

2. In evaluating the impact of a public outreach campaign, the _____ model can be used early in the campaign to address first impressions. 2.____
   A. exposure or advertising
   B. expert interview
   C. impact monitoring or process
   D. experimental or quasi-experimental

3. When trying to motivate an older population to take action on a community problem, it is helpful to remember that older people 3.____
   A. are more self-reliant in their decision-making than other members of the same family
   B. often need more time to decide than younger people
   C. are more likely than younger people to view community problems self-referentially
   D. tend to take a pragmatic, rather than philosophical, view of life

4. The method of group or community decision-making that is normally MOST time-consuming is 4.____
   A. majority opinion
   B. consensus
   C. expert opinion
   D. authority rule

5. A local adult protective services agency has identified one of the goals of its recent public outreach campaign to be the mobilization of activists. 5.____
The campaign should probably
   A. target neutral audiences
   B. home in on supporters
   C. stick to purely factual information
   D. try to persuade community fence-sitters

6. Research of Native American youths' perceptions of family concerns for their well-being has generally found that these youths 6.____
   A. have a high degree of uncertainty about their families' feelings toward them
   B. believe their families don't care about them
   C. believe that their mothers care a great deal about them, but their fathers don't
   D. believe their families care a great deal about them

7. A domestic violence specialist is developing a new outreach program for the local community. The specialist has defined the target problem, set program goals, and planned the actions that will take place as a result of the program. Most likely, the next step will be to 7.____
   A. evaluate the resources available to achieve program goals
   B. define and sequence the steps that will be taken to achieve program goals
   C. determine how the program will evaluated
   D. decide how the program will operate

8. Elder: *I'm so glad to have someone to talk to, someone who really understands my problem.* 8.____
   Specialist: *It is nice to be able to talk to someone who will listen.*
   Elder: *That's for sure.*
   In the above exchange, what listening skill is evident in the underlined statement?
   A. Verbatim response
   B. Paraphrasing
   C. Advising
   D. Evaluation

9. Which of the following activities is involved in the specialist's task of mobilizing? 9.____
   A. Meeting individuals in the community with problems and assisting them in finding help
   B. Identifying unmet community needs
   C. Speaking out against an unjust policy or procedure
   D. Developing new services or linking presently available services to meet community needs

10. The preliminary research associated with a public outreach campaign should FIRST be aimed at determining 10.____
   A. the budget
   B. the message's ultimate audience
   C. what media to use
   D. the short-term behavioral goals of the campaign

11. A specialist in a low-income community wants to plan programs that will deal with the influence of unemployment on domestic disturbances. The specialist needs to know not only how many unemployed people are in the community now, but also how many people will be unemployed at any particular tie in the future, and how those numbers will vary given certain conditions. 11.____

Probably the BEST way to trace employment rates over time and within differing conditions is through the use of

A. the critical path
B. linear programming
C. difference equations
D. the Markov model

12. Generally, public outreach programs—whatever their stated goal—should 12.____

I. create a sense of urgency about a problem
II. decline to identify opponents of the issue or idea
III. propose concrete, easily understandable solutions
IV. urge a specific action

The CORRECT answer is:

A. I only
B. I, III and IV
C. II and III
D. I, II, III and IV

13. Which of the following methods of community needs assessment relies to the GREATEST degree on existing public records? 13.____

A. Social indicators
B. Field study
C. Rates under treatment
D. Key informant

14. During an interview with a Native American client, a specialist is careful to maintain close and nearly constant eye contact. 14.____
The client is MOST likely to interpret this as a(n)

A. show of high concern
B. sign of disrespect
C. uncomfortable assumption of intimacy
D. attempt to intimidate

15. The BEST strategy for addressing an audience that is known to be captive, or even hostile, is to 15.____

A. refer to experiences in common
B. flatter the audience
C. joke about things in or near the audience
D. plead for fairness

16. Integrative conflict resolution is characterized by 16.____

A. an overriding concern to maximize joint outcomes
B. one side's interests opposing the other's
C. a fixed and limited amount of resources to be divided, so that the more one group gets, the less another gets
D. manipulation and withholding information as negotiation strategies

17. A specialist wants to learn how to interact with the members of a largely Latino community in a more culturally sensitive way. 17.____
Which of the following is NOT a guideline for interacting with members of a Latino community?

A. Efforts to foster independence and self-reliance may be interpreted by many Latinos as a lack of concern for others.
B. Efforts to deal one-on-one with an adolescent client may serve to alienate the parents, especially the mother.

C. A nonverbal gesture, such as lowering the eyes, is interpreted by many Latinos as a sign of respect and deference to authority.
D. In much of Latino culture, the focus of control for problems tends to be much more external than internal.

18. Each of the following is a supporting assumption of community organization, EXCEPT: 18.____
A. Democracy requires cooperative participation.
B. In order for communities to change, it is necessary for each individual in the community to be willing to change.
C. Communities often need help with organization and planning.
D. Holistic approaches work better than fragmented or ad-hoc programs.

19. Helping professionals often have difficulty to bring community resources together to fulfill unmet community needs. 19.____
Which of the following is NOT usually a reason for this?
A. Some community groups resist assistance when it is offered.
B. Few community groups make their needs known.
C. Community resources frequently change the type of services they offer.
D. Often, community resources prefer to work alone.

20. When dealing with groups or populations of elderly clients, specialists should be mindful that about _____ of the nation's elderly suffer from mental health problems. 20.____
A. a tenth B. a quarter C. a third D. half

21. In an African-American community, a specialist from another culture should recognize that church participation, for most African-Americans, is viewed as a 21.____
A. method for maintaining control and communicating competency
B. way of depersonalizing problems or troubles
C. way to divert attention away from problems
D. means of cathartic emotional release

22. Adult protective service programs supported by state statutes protect elderly people from abuse and neglect under the doctrine of 22.____
A. parens patriae B. habeas corpus
C. in loco parentis D. volenti non fit injuria

23. In terms of public outreach, which of the following statements about an audience is NOT generally true? 23.____
A. The more heterogeneous the audience, the more necessary it will be to use specific examples and appeals to certain types of people.
B. The smaller the audience, the more likely that its members will share assumptions and values.
C. When the speaker does not know the status of an audience, it is best to assume that they are captive rather than voluntary.
D. The larger an audience, the more formal a presentation is likely to be.

24. A specialist often spends time in the places frequented by community residents. She listens carefully to what residents seem most concerned about, and engages many in conversations, asking them how they see the problems in the community. During these conversations, she makes mental notes about whether the statements of the problems are the same things that are mentioned in their conversations. From these conversations, the worker determines what she thinks the unmet needs of the community are. Which of the key issues in identifying unmet needs has the worker neglected to address? 24.____
    A. The different points of view regarding the issues, and whether there is any common ground
    B. Whether the stated problems and conversations with community residents reflect the same concerns
    C. How community residents define the issues
    D. What the residents talk about with one another in a community

25. Which of the following political styles should be used to promote an issue that could become controversial if it is perceived to involve major reforms? 25.____
    A. High-conflict, polarized
    B. High-conflict, consensual
    C. Moderate conflict, compromise-oriented
    D. Low-conflict, technical

KEY (CORRECT ANSWERS)

1.	C	11.	D
2.	A	12.	B
3.	B	13.	A
4.	B	14.	B
5.	B	15.	A
6.	D	16.	A
7.	A	17.	D
8.	B	18.	B
9.	D	19.	C
10.	B	20.	B

21. D
22. A
23. A
24. A
25. D

COMMUNICATION

EXAMINATION SECTION
TEST 1

DIRECTIONS: Each question or incomplete statement is followed by several suggested answers or completions. Select the one that BEST answers the question or completes the statement. *PRINT THE LETTER OF THE CORRECT ANSWER IN THE SPACE AT THE RIGHT.*

1. In some agencies the counsel to the agency head is given the right to bypass the chain of command and issue orders directly to the staff concerning matters that involve certain specific processes and practices. 1.____
   This situation MOST nearly illustrates the principle of _____ authority.
   A. the acceptance theory of
   B. multiple-linear
   C. splintered
   D. functional

2. It is commonly understood that communication is an important part of the administrative process. 2.____
   Which of the following is NOT a valid principle of the communication process in administration?
   A. The channels of communication should be spontaneous.
   B. The lines of communication should be as direct and as short as possible.
   C. Communications should be authenticated.
   D. The persons serving in communications centers should be competent.

3. Of the following, the one factor which is generally considered LEAST essential to successful committee operations is 3.____
   A. stating a clear definition of the authority and scope of the committee
   B. selecting the committee chairman carefully
   C. limiting the size of the committee to four persons
   D. limiting the subject matter to that which can be handled in group discussion

4. Of the following, the failure by line managers to accept and appreciate the benefits and limitations of a new program or system VERY FREQUENTLY can be traced to the 4.____
   A. budgetary problems involved
   B. resultant need to reduce staff
   C. lack of controls it engenders
   D. failure of top management to support its implementation

5. If a manager were thinking about using a committee of subordinates to solve an operating problem, which of the following would generally NOT be an advantage of such use of the committee approach? 5.____
   A. Improved coordination
   B. Low cost
   C. Increased motivation
   D. Integrated judgment

6. Every supervisor has many occasions to lead a conference or participate in a conference of some sort. 6.____
Of the following statements that pertain to conferences and conference leadership, which is generally considered to be MOST valid?
   A. Since World War II, the trend has been toward fewer shared decisions and more conferences.
   B. The most important part of a conference leader's job is to direct discussion.
   C. In providing opportunities for group interaction, management should avoid consideration of its past management philosophy.
   D. A good administrator cannot lead a good conference if he is a poor public speaker.

7. Of the following, it is usually LEAST desirable for a conference leader to 7.____
   A. call the name of a person after asking a question
   B. summarize proceedings periodically
   C. make a practice of repeating questions
   D. ask a question without indicating who is to reply

8. Assume that, in a certain organization, a situation has developed in which there is little difference in status or authority between individuals. 8.____
Which of the following would be the MOST likely result with regard to communication in this organization?
   A. Both the accuracy and flow of communication will be improved.
   B. Both the accuracy and flow of communication will substantially decrease.
   C. Employees will seek more formal lines of communication.
   D. Neither the flow nor the accuracy of communication will be improved over the former hierarchical structure.

9. The main function of many agency administrative officers is "information management." Information that is received by an administrative officer may be classified as active or passive, depending upon whether or not it requires the recipient to take some action. 9.____
Of the following, the item received which is clearly the MOST active information is
   A. an appointment of a new staff member
   B. a payment voucher for a new desk
   C. a press release concerning a past event
   D. the minutes of a staff meeting

10. Of the following, the one LEAST considered to be a communication barrier is 10.____
   A. group feedback
   B. charged words
   C. selective perception
   D. symbolic meanings

11. Management studies support the hypothesis that, in spite of the tendency of employees to censor the information communicated to their supervisor, subordinates are more likely to communicate problem-oriented information UPWARD when they have a 11.____
   A. long period of service in the organization
   B. high degree of trust in the supervisor
   C. high educational level
   D. low status on the organizational ladder

12. Electronic data processing equipment can produce more information faster than can be generated by any other means. 12.____
In view of this, the MOST important problem faced by management at present is to
   A. keep computers fully occupied
   B. find enough computer personnel
   C. assimilate and properly evaluate the information
   D. obtain funds to establish appropriate information systems

13. A well-designed management information system essentially provides each executive and manager the information he needs for 13.____
   A. determining computer time requirements
   B. planning and measuring results
   C. drawing a new organization chart
   D. developing a new office layout

14. It is generally agreed that management policies should be periodically reappraised and restated in accordance with current conditions. 14.____
Of the following, the approach which would be MOST effective in determining whether a policy should be revised is to
   A. conduct interviews with staff members at all levels in order to ascertain the relationship between the policy and actual practice
   B. make proposed revisions in the policy and apply it to current problems
   C. make up hypothetical situations using both the old policy and a revised version in order to make comparisons
   D. call a meeting of top level staff in order to discuss ways of revising the policy

15. Your superior has asked you to notify division employees of an important change in one of the operating procedures described in the division manual. Every employee presently has a copy of this manual. 15.____
Which of the following is normally the MOST practical way to get the employees to understand such a change?
   A. Notify each employee individually of the change and answer any questions he might have
   B. Send a written notice to key personnel, directing them to inform the people under them

C. Call a general meeting, distribute a corrected page for the manual, and discuss the change
D. Send a memo to employees describing the change in general terms and asking them to make the necessary corrections in their copies of the manual

16. Assume that the work in your department involves the use of any technical terms. 16.____
In such a situation, when you are answering inquiries from the general public, it would usually be BEST to
A. use simple language and avoid the technical terms
B. employ the technical terms whenever possible
C. bandy technical terms freely, but explain each term in parentheses
D. apologize if you are forced to use a technical term

17. Suppose that you receive a telephone call from someone identifying himself as an employee in another city department who asks to be given information which your own department regards as confidential. 17.____
Which of the following is the BEST way of handling such a request?
A. Give the information requested, since your caller as official standing
B. Grant the request, provided the caller gives you a signed receipt
C. Refuse the request, because you have no way of knowing whether the caller is really who he claims to be
D. Explain that the information is confidential and inform the caller of the channels he must go through to have the information released to him

18. Studies show that office employees place high importance on the social and human aspects of the organization. What office employees like best about their jobs is the kind of people with whom they work. So strive hard to group people who are most likely to get along well together. 18.____
Based on this information, it is MOST reasonable to assume that office workers are most pleased to work in a group which
A. is congenial
B. has high productivity
C. allows individual creativity
D. is unlike other groups

19. A certain supervisor does not compliment members of his staff when they come up with good ideas. He feels that coming up with good ideas is part of the job and does not merit special attention. 19.____
This supervisor's practice is
A. *poor*, because recognition for good ideas is a good motivator
B. *poor*, because the staff will suspect that the supervisor has no good ideas of his own
C. *good*, because it is reasonable to assume that employees will tell their supervisor of ways to improve office practice
D. *good*, because the other members of the staff are not made to seem inferior by comparison

20. Some employees of a department have sent an anonymous letter containing many complaints to the department head. 20.____
Of the following, what is this MOST likely to show about the department?
   A. It is probably a good place to work.
   B. Communications are probably poor.
   C. The complaints are probably unjustified.
   D. These employees are probably untrustworthy.

21. Which of the following actions would usually be MOST appropriate for a supervisor to take after receiving an instruction sheet from his superior explaining a new procedure which is to be followed? 21.____
   A. Put the instruction sheet aside temporarily until he determines what is wrong with the old procedure.
   B. Call his superior and ask whether the procedure is one he must implement immediately.
   C. Write a memorandum to the superior asking for more details.
   D. Try the new procedure and advise the superior of any problems or possible improvements.

22. Of the following, which one is considered the PRIMARY advantage of using a committee to resolved a problem in an organization? 22.____
   A. No one person will be held accountable for the decision since a group of people was involved.
   B. People with different backgrounds give attention to the problem.
   C. The decision will take considerable time so there is unlikely to be a decision that will later be regretted.
   D. One person cannot dominate the decision-making process.

23. Employees in a certain office come to their supervisor with all their complaints about the office and the work. Almost every employee has had at least one minor complaint at some time. 23.____
The situation with respect to complaints in this office may BEST be described as probably
   A. *good*; employees who complain care about their jobs and work hard
   B. *good*; grievances brought out into the open can be corrected
   C. *bad*; only serious complaints should be discussed
   D. *bad*; it indicates the staff does not have confidence in the administration

24. The administrator who allows his staff to suggest ways to do their work will usually find that 24.____
   A. this practice contributes to high productivity
   B. the administrator's ideas produce greater output
   C. clerical employees suggest inefficient work methods
   D. subordinate employees resent performing a management function

25. The MAIN purpose for a supervisor's questioning the employees at a conference he is holding is to 25.____
   A. stress those areas of information covered but not understood by the participants
   B. encourage participants to think through the problem under discussion
   C. catch those subordinates who are not paying attention
   D. permit the more knowledgeable participants to display their grasp of the problems being discussed

---

KEY (CORRECT ANSWERS)

1. D
2. A
3. C
4. D
5. B

6. B
7. C
8. D
9. A
10. A

11. B
12. C
13. B
14. A
15. C

16. A
17. D
18. A
19. A
20. B

21. D
22. B
23. B
24. A
25. B

TEST 2

DIRECTIONS: Each question or incomplete statement is followed by several suggested answers or completions. Select the one that BEST answers the question or completes the statement. *PRINT THE LETTER OF THE CORRECT ANSWER IN THE SPACE AT THE RIGHT.*

1. For a superior to use *consultative supervision* with his subordinates effectively, it is ESSENTIAL that he 1.____
   A. accept the fact that his formal authority will be weakened by the procedure
   B. admit that he does not know more than all his men together and that his ideas are not always best
   C. utilize a committee system so that the procedure is orderly
   D. make sure that all subordinates are consulted so that no one feels left out

2. The *grapevine* is an informal means of communication in an organization. The attitude of a supervisor with respect to the grapevine should be to 2.____
   A. ignore it since it deals mainly with rumors and sensational information
   B. regard it as a serious danger which should be eliminated
   C. accept it as a real line of communication which should be listened to
   D. utilize it for most purposes instead of the official line of communication

3. The supervisor of an office that must deal with the public should realize that planning in this type of work situation 3.____
   A. is useless because he does not know how many people will request service or what service they will request
   B. must be done at a higher level but that he should be ready to implement the results of such planning
   C. is useful primarily for those activities that are not concerned with public contact
   D. is useful for all the activities of the office, including those that relate to public contact

4. Assume that it is your job to receive incoming telephone calls. Those calls which you cannot handle yourself have to be transferred to the appropriate office. 4.____
   If you receive an outside call for an extension line which is busy, the one of the following which you should do FIRST is to
   A. interrupt the person speaking on the extension and tell him a call is waiting
   B. tell the caller the line is busy and let him know every thirty seconds whether or not it is free
   C. leave the caller on "hold" until the extension is free
   D. tell the caller the line is busy and ask him if he wishes to wait

5. Your superior has subscribed to several publications directly related to your division's work, and he has asked you to see to it that the publications are circulated among the supervisory personnel in the division. There are eight supervisors involved. 5.____
The BEST method of insuring that all eight see these publications is to
   A. place the publication in the division's general reference library as soon as it arrives
   B. inform each supervisor whenever a publication arrives and remind all of them that they are responsible for reading it
   C. prepare a standard slip that can be stapled to each publication, listing the eight supervisors and saying, "Please read, initial your name, and pass along"
   D. send a memo to the eight supervisors saying that they may wish to purchase individual subscriptions in their own names if they are interested in seeing each issue

6. Your superior has telephoned a number of key officials in your agency to ask whether they can meet at a certain time next month. He has found that they can all make it, and he has asked you to confirm the meeting. 6.____
Which of the following is the BEST way to confirm such a meeting?
   A. Note the meeting on your superior's calendar.
   B. Post a notice of the meeting on the agency bulletin board.
   C. Call the officials on the day of the meeting to remind them of the meeting.
   D. Write a memo to each official involved, repeating the time and place of the meeting.

7. Assume that a new city regulation requires that certain kinds of private organizations file information forms with your department. You have been asked to write the short explanatory message that will be printed on the front cover of the pamphlet containing the forms and instructions. 7.____
Which of the following would be the MOST appropriate way of beginning this message?
   A. Get the readers' attention by emphasizing immediately that there are legal penalties for organizations that fail to file before a certain date.
   B. Briefly state the nature of the enclosed forms and the types of organizations that must file.
   C. Say that your department is very sorry to have to put organizations to such an inconvenience.
   D. Quote the entire regulation adopted by the city, even if it is quite long and is expressed din complicated legal language.

8. Suppose that you have been told to make up the vacation schedule for the 18 employees in a particular unit. In order for the unit to operate effectively, only a few employees can be on vacation at the same time. 8.____
Which of the following is the MOST advisable approach in making up the schedule?
   A. Draw up a schedule assigning vacations in alphabetical order
   B. Find out when the supervisors want to take their vacations, and randomly assign whatever periods are left to the non-supervisory personnel

C. Assign the most desirable times to employees of longest standing and the least desirable times to the newest employees
D. Have all employees state their own preference, and then work out any conflicts in consultation with the people involved

9. Assume that you have been asked to prepare job descriptions for various positions in your department. 9.____
Which of the following are the basic points that should be covered in a *job description*?
A. General duties and responsibilities of the position, with examples of day-to-day tasks
B. Comments on the performances of present employees
C. Estimates of the number of openings that may be available in each category during the coming year
D. Instructions for carrying out the specific tasks assigned to your department

10. Of the following, the biggest DISADVANTAGE in allowing a free flow of communications in an agency is that such a free flow 10.____
A. decreases creativity
B. increases the use of the *grapevine*
C. lengthens the chain of command
D. reduces the executive's power to direct the flow of information

11. A downward flow of authority in an organization is one example of _____ communication. 11.____
A. horizontal B. informal C. circular D. vertical

12. Of the following, the one that would MOST likely block effective communication is 12.____
A. concentration only on the issues at hand
B. lack of interest or commitment
C. use of written reports
D. use of charts and graphs

13. An ADVANTAGE of the *lecture* as a teaching tool is that it 13.____
A. enables a person to present his ideas to a large number of people
B. allows the audience to retain a maximum of the information given
C. holds the attention of the audience for the longest time
D. enables the audience member to easily recall the main points

14. An ADVANTAGE of the *small-group* discussion as a teaching tool is that 14.____
A. it always focuses attention on one person as the leader
B. it places collective responsibility on the group as a whole
C. its members gain experience by summarizing the ideas of others
D. each member of the group acts as a member of a team

15. The one of the following that is an ADVANTAGE of a *large-group* discussion, when compared to a small-group discussion, is that the large-group discussion 15.____
    A. moves along more quickly than a small-group discussion
    B. allows its participants to feel more at ease, and speak out more freely
    C. gives the whole group a chance to exchange ideas on a certain subject at the same occasion
    D. allows its members to feel a greater sense of personal responsibility

KEY (CORRECT ANSWERS)

1.	D	6.	D	11.	D
2.	C	7.	B	12.	B
3.	D	8.	D	13.	A
4.	D	9.	A	14.	D
5.	C	10.	D	15.	C

EXAMINATION SECTION

TEST 1

DIRECTIONS: Each question or incomplete statement is followed by several suggested answers or completions. Select the one that BEST answers the question or completes the statement. *PRINT THE LETTER OF THE CORRECT ANSWER IN THE SPACE AT THE RIGHT.*

1. Managing conflict effectively by avoiding no-win situations, positively influencing the actions of others and using _____ strategies are what make a great leader. 1.____
   A. persuasive B. ambiguous C. prosecution D. performance

2. In today's business world, collaboration will bring together people from distinct backgrounds. These collaborative groups may not share common norms, morals or _____, but they can offer unique _____. 2.____
   A. vocabulary; perspectives B. salaries; vocabulary
   C. modifications; insights D. perspectives; salaries

3. E-mail is a great tool for communication; however, which of the following should you be careful of when in electronic communication with a colleague? 3.____
   A. Font size B. E-mail length
   C. Font color D. Tone of voice

4. A formal relationship can BEST be described as 4.____
   A. regulated by procedures or directives
   B. personal and relaxed
   C. emotionally distant and very uncomfortable
   D. confusing and unproductive

5. John is in a meeting with his supervisor ad coworkers. He is thinking about what he's going to have for dinner that night when his boss asks him a question. John can repeat back what his supervisor said, but he cannot retain what was said during the meeting. 5.____
   This is a classic example of failing to
   A. focus at work
   B. effectively listen
   C. leave personal plans outside the workplace
   D. care about meetings

6. A person's choice of _____ can directly affect communication. 6.____
   A. clothing B. food C. hygiene D. words

7. Why is it important to relax when communicating with team members? 7.____
   A. Relaxing always means having better ideas.
   B. People will automatically like you more if you are relaxed.

C. If you are nervous, you may talk too quickly and make it hard for others to understand your message or directive.
D. No one likes someone who is always working, so it is important to relax and not work too hard.

8. In order to show you are genuinely interested in what others have to say, you should 8.____
   A. tell them how nice they are
   B. repeat what they say back to them
   C. nod and find something to compliment them about
   D. ask questions and seek clarification from them

9. Jack and James are always arguing with one another. Their supervisor calls each one in separately to talk to them. He asks Jack to think about things from James' point of view and he asks James to do the same for Jack. 9.____
   What is the supervisor trying to get each person to do?
   A. Get along B. Be positive
   C. Communicate effectively D. Empathize

10. When working in groups, disagreements 10.____
    A. should be avoided at all costs
    B. are often a healthy way of building understanding and camaraderie
    C. lead coworkers to hate one another and the company they work for
    D. don't happen if the supervisor chooses the right people to work together

11. If things go wrong in a group situation, it is important to AVOID 11.____
    A. the boss B. disagreements or arguments
    C. scapegoating D. being polite and fair to one another

12. If you are a listener who likes to hear the rationale behind a message, your listening style would be described as _____ style. 12.____
    A. results B. process C. reasons D. eye contact

13. Which of the following BEST describes a psychological barrier in communication? 13.____
    A. Molly is so stressed about her paying for her mortgage that she can't focus at work right now.
    B. John doesn't understand a lot of the terms the IT specialist used in an e-mail sent out to everyone.
    C. Jerry is a little older and has a hard time hearing everything so sometimes he misses parts of a conversation.
    D. Linda doesn't want to be at the company for longer than a few months, so she doesn't really try too hard to fit in.

14. Body language, also known as _____, is really important when building rapport with coworkers and communicating effectively. 14.____
    A. verbal language B. kinesthetic
    C. non-verbal communication D. facial expressions

15. Which of the following might be a good example of someone who has a "closed" posture? 15.____
    A. Hands are apart on the arms of the chair.
    B. His/her arms are folded.
    C. They are directly facing you.
    D. They barely speak above a whisper.

16. Which of the following can eye contact be used for? 16.____
    A. To give and receive feedback
    B. To let someone know when it is their turn to speak
    C. To communicate how you feel about someone
    D. All of the above

17. Which of the following is NOT a form of non-verbal communication? 17.____
    A. Crossing your arms when talking to someone
    B. Using space within the room in a conversation
    C. Clearing your throat before you speak]
    D. Saying "10-4" when asked if you understand

18. Your best friend has just been hired at the company you work for. You notice he has come into work on several occasions after staying out late the night before. His work has not suffered yet, but you fear it will. 18.____
    Which of the following actions should you take to help prevent future problems?
    A. Do nothing; he's your friend but it is his life
    B. Try to talk to him and help him see the importance of not creating bad habits.
    C. Talk to your supervisor and tell him your friend isn't suitable for the job
    D. Tell your friend to change his ways or to quit

19. Interacting with coworkers can be positively or negatively affected by _____ when someone's previous biases and assumptions shape their reactions in future situations. 19.____
    A. racism B. past experience
    C. interpersonal skills D. active listening

20. Which of the following scenarios BEST describes a person who is being subjective? 20.____
    A. Sally is fair and honest when she listens to coworkers. She does not take sides and wants the best solution to the problem.
    B. Mike doesn't like Steve, because he thinks Steve is only out for himself. Still, Steve offers valuable insights, so Mike tries not to let personal feelings get in the way of working together.
    C. Jamie is dating Veronica's ex and Veronica just found out. Now, Veronica immediately shoots down anything Jamie suggests during a meeting as irrational and superfluous.
    D. None of the above

21. Which important communications tem is MOST closely defined as "the quality of a sound governed by the rate of vibrations producing it; the degree of highness or lowness of a tone"? 21.____
    A. Tone B. Pitch
    C. Effective communication D. Rationalization

22. _____ is when a person tries to make an imprudent and reckless action seem reasonable. 22.____
    A. Projection B. Self-deception
    C. Past experience D. Rationalization

23. When holding conversations with coworkers, you should 23.____
    A. do most of the talking
    B. let others do most of the talking
    C. try to split time between talking and listening
    D. zone out and wait for the meeting to finish

24. A new hire just arrived and you are meeting her for the first time. Which of the following actions is MOST appropriate? 24.____
    A. Walk up and introduce yourself with a smile and a handshake
    B. Wait for her to come and introduce herself
    C. Approach her and offer a hug to make her feel welcome
    D. Ignore the new hire; she is likely your competition

25. If you are the type of listener who likes to discuss concepts or issues in detail, you would MOST likely fall under which listening style? 25.____
    A. Process B. Reasons
    C. Results D. None of the above

KEY (CORRECT ANSWERS)

1. A
2. A
3. D
4. A
5. B

6. D
7. C
8. D
9. D
10. B

11. C
12. C
13. A
14. C
15. B

16. D
17. D
18. B
19. B
20. C

21. B
22. D
23. C
24. A
25. A

TEST 2

DIRECTIONS: Each question or incomplete statement is followed by several suggested answers or completions. Select the one that BEST answers the question or completes the statement. *PRINT THE LETTER OF THE CORRECT ANSWER IN THE SPACE AT THE RIGHT.*

1. Which of the following is an example of the BEST practice when communicating in the workplace? 1.____
   A. You are horrible with remembering names so you try to use nicknames to cover up for your poor memory.
   B. You only pay attention to the names of people who you work for or who you deem to be "important."
   C. You try to remember everyone's names and use them whenever possible.
   D. None of the above

2. Words of civility such as "please" and "thank you" should be used _____ when conversing with coworkers and business partners. 2.____
   A. always B. sometimes C. rarely D. never

3. When communicating with others, one should _____ stand as close to them as possible and make body contact in order to get an important point across. 3.____
   A. always B. sometimes C. rarely D. never

4. The MOST appropriate way to end a conversation is to 4.____
   A. seek a mutual resolution, but leave abruptly if it continues
   B. find a way to wrap up the conversation so the other person knows it is time to move on
   C. look impatient so hopefully the person will get the hint
   D. tell the other person the conversation should end

5. Another name for interpersonal communication in an office setting is 5.____
   A. peer-to-peer communication B. mass communication
   C. virtual reality D. e-mailing

6. Of the following statements, choose the one you feel is the MOST correct. 6.____
   A. Devoid of interpersonal communication, people become sick.
   B. Communication is not completely needed for humans.
   C. People are the only animals that need to have relationships in order to survive.
   D. Important communication is not really relevant until after you become an adult.

7. John is giving a presentation on ways to communicate effectively with peers. He is having trouble deciding on what to say in his speech. Which of the following statements should he AVOID using? 7.____
   A. Always try to understand another person's point of view or perspective
   B. Try to imagine what someone is going to say before they actually say it

C. Be aware of how non-verbal cues like eye contact and body language affect how your message is received
D. Both B and C

8. Which of the following would MOST affect our perception of communication with coworkers? 8.____
A. Past experiences B. Marital problems
C. Rumors spread about coworkers D. None of the above

9. Many people think of communication as both _____ and _____ messages. 9.____
A. formal; informal B. hearing; listening
C. sending; receiving D. finding; decoding

10. Why is context important in communication? 10.____
A. It's important to know which buttons to push in order to get what you want.
B. Saying something to one person may not have the same effect as saying it to someone else.
C. Context is only important if you are worried about what others think.
D. None of the above

11. If your brother is normally bright and talkative during the summer, but you notice he gets quiet and subdued in the winter, the MOST likely communication context he is dealing with would be 11.____
A. relational B. cultural C. inner D. physical

12. _____ is an example of a negative nonverbal action you can take. 12.____
A. Smiling
B. Using a tone of voice that matches your message
C. Maintaining eye contact
D. Slumping your shoulders

13. Cultural context can BEST be described as 13.____
A. what people think of as it relates to the event they are participating in (i.e., wedding versus a funeral)
B. the connection between a father and his son
C. rules and patterns of Americans versus the Japanese
D. thoughts, feelings, and sensations inside a person's head

14. Which of the following BEST describes feedback? 14.____
A. Staring at the speaker while he talks
B. Nodding and smiling while listening to a speaker
C. Standing an appropriate distance away so the speaker does not get uncomfortable
D. Trying to speak while the other person is speaking because you have something more important to say

15. Being able to communicate more effectively can be improved upon by 15.____
    A. continually making an effort to be as flexible as possible when talking to others
    B. committing to one style of speaking until you master it
    C. using the same style of correspondence as the person with whom you are speaking
    D. always using the opposite style of communication from the person you are speaking to

16. John walks up to Sally and compliments her on the dress she wore to work today. In his mind, John was just being friendly, but Sally went to her manager and filed a harassment charge against John. 16.____
    This miscommunication could MOST easily be classified as an error in what?
    A. Reality B. Perception C. Friendship D. Loyalty

17. If a speaker's tone is flat and monotone, which of the following is the MOST likely reaction that listeners will have? 17.____
    They will
    A. enthused by the message
    B. enjoy the message but not be overly excited about it
    C. be polite and interested but will not seem very engaged
    D. be bored and uninterested in the message

18. When Steve speaks to his group about his ideas, he generally has a higher pitch to his voice and gesticulates frequently. 18.____
    This lead his team members to believe that Steve
    A. is enthusiastic and has great ideas for the group
    B. has had too much caffeine and needs to relax
    C. is trying to show off for the boss and make them look bad
    D. is extremely smart and great at his job

19. _____ is used when a person wants to add stress to key words in communication. It lets the audience understand the mood or feelings of particular words or phrases. 19.____
    A. Anger B. Tone C. Perception D. Inflection

20. If Barry tells Bill that his haircut looks "great" and Bill can tell Barry is being insincere, which of the following tones is Barry MOST likely using? 20.____
    A. Affectionate B. Apologetic C. Threatening D. Sarcastic

21. As a supervisor, it is important that everyone clearly comprehends everything you communicate to them. 21.____
    In order to ensure this happens, which of the following things should you avoid?
    A. Overusing jargon
    B. Explaining something more than once
    C. Speaking slowly and annunciating everything
    D. Having meetings in the morning

22. If your supervisor is looking down at the ground or has his back to you as he is speaking, it MOST clearly indicates to those who are listening to him that the supervisor 22.____
    A. is shy and doesn't like speaking in front of people
    B. is disinterested and doesn't care what he's talking about
    C. is approachable and friendly
    D. dislikes his job and wants to get out as soon as possible

23. Interpersonal communication helps you 23.____
    A. know what others are thinking
    B. turn into an inspiring speaker, especially in public
    C. learn about yourself
    D. communicate with the general public

24. In general, people who smile more are perceived as 24.____
    A. devious
    B. friendly
    C. attractive
    D. easy to manipulate

25. If your supervisor constantly takes advantage of you and expresses his or her opinion often at the expense of you or other workers, which communication style are they MOST likely using? 25.____
    A. Nonassertive
    B. Assertive
    C. Aggressive
    D. Peacemaking

KEY (CORRECT ANSWERS)

1.	C	11.	D
2.	A	12.	D
3.	D	13.	C
4.	B	14.	B
5.	A	15.	A
6.	A	16.	B
7.	B	17.	D
8.	A	18.	A
9.	C	19.	D
10.	B	20.	D

21.	A
22.	B
23.	D
24.	B
25.	C

EXAMINATION SECTION

TEST 1

DIRECTIONS: Each question or incomplete statement is followed by several suggested answers or completions. Select the one that BEST answers the question or completes the statement. *PRINT THE LETTER OF THE CORRECT ANSWER IN THE SPACE AT THE RIGHT.*

1. Assume that you are a supervisor recently assigned to a new unit. You notice that, for the past few days, one of the employees in your unit whose work is about average has been stopping work at about four o'clock and has been spending the rest of the afternoon relaxing at his desk. 1.____
The BEST of the following actions for you to take in this situation is to
   A. assign more work to this employee since it is apparent that he does not have enough work to keep him busy
   B. observe the employee's conduct more closely for about ten days before taking any more positive action
   C. discuss the matter with the employee, pointing out to him how he can use the extra hour daily to raise the level of his job performance
   D. question the previous supervisor in charge of the unit in order to determine whether he had sanctioned such conduct when he supervised that unit

2. A supervisor, newly assigned in charge of a small project, discovers that the previous supervisor and one of the employees supervised by him put all their business communications with each other in written form. The newly assigned supervisor finds that the employee is continuing to put his communications in writing and has requested that the supervisor do the same in order to prevent misunderstandings. 2.____
It would generally be BEST for the supervisor to
   A. accede to the request since the likelihood of misunderstandings will be reduced and since, as a newly assigned supervisor, he should not make changes until he is well established and accepted
   B. allow the employee to communicate with him in the way in which he chooses but refuse to communicate with the employee in writing except in cases where he would generally consider written communications to be desirable, on the grounds that too much of the supervisor's time would be wasted thereby
   C. inform the employee that neither one of them is to use written communications excessively in order to reduce the time consumed by communication but with the understanding that the employee may resort to writing in cases where he has serious reason to fear a misunderstanding
   D. instruct the employee to cease the use of written communications in excess of the use of them by the other employees and refuses to accede to his request since the result would be an excessive waste of time

3. A policy of direct crosswise communication on a project between a member of the management staff and a member of the maintenance staff of equal or superior status rather than following the chain of command upward through the manager and down through the top maintenance supervisor is a policy to be 2.____
   A. *discouraged*, primarily because it places responsibility where it does not belong and makes the quality of communication erratic and undependable
   B. *discouraged*, primarily because the manager and upper level supervisors will fail to receive the full information they need to make policy and administrative decisions
   C. *encouraged*, primarily because it results in decision making at the lowest practical level
   D. *encouraged*, primarily because it shortens the communication time and improves the quality of communication

4. A supervisor in a large department should be thoroughly familiar with modern methods of personnel administration. This statement is 4.____
   A. *true*, because this familiarity will help him in performing the normal functions of his office
   B. *false*, because in a large city personnel administration is not a departmental matter, but is centralized in a civil service commission
   C. *true*, because this knowledge will insure the elimination of personnel problems in a department
   D. *false*, because the departmental problems of a minor character are handled by the personnel representative, while major problems are the responsibility of the commissioner

5. The LEAST true of the following is that a supervisor in a large department 5.____
   A. executes the policy laid down by the commissioner or his deputies
   B. in the main, carries out the policies of the commissioner but with some leeway where his own frame of reference is determinative
   C. is never required to formulate policy
   D. is responsible for the successful accomplishment of a section of the department's program

6. In the supervision of young inexperienced investigators, the MOST important training task for the supervisor is to 6.____
   A. encourage investigators to make their own decisions about case problems
   B. give experience-based answers to various problems that arise in cases
   C. teach investigators how to analyze and assess important facts in order to make decisions about case problems
   D. teach investigators how to recognize evidence of mental breakdown

7. The supervisor is responsible for the accuracy of the work performed by his subordinates. Of the following procedures which he might adopt to insure the accurate copying of long reports from rough draft originals, the MOST effective one is to 7.____
   A. examine the rough draft for errors in grammar, punctuation, and spelling before assigning it to a typist to copy

B. glance through each typed report before it leaves his bureau to detect any obvious errors made by the typist
C. have another employee read the rough draft original to the typist who typed the report, and have the typist make whatever corrections are necessary
D. rotate assignments involving the typing of long reports equally among all the typists in the unit

8. In the course of your duties, you receive a letter which, you believe, should be called to the attention of your superior. 8.____
Of the following, the BEST reason for attaching previous correspondence to this letter before giving it to your superior is that
A. there is less danger, if such a procedure is followed, of misplacing important letters
B. this letter can probably be better understood in the light of previous correspondence
C. your supervisor is probably in a better position to understand the letter than you
D. this letter will have to be filed eventually so there is no additional work involved

9. The most successful supervisor wins his victories through preventive rather than through curative action. 9.____
The one of the following which is the MOST accurate statement on the basis of this counsel is that
A. success in supervision may be measured more accurately in terms of errors corrected than in terms of errors prevented
B. anticipating problems makes for better supervision than waiting until problems arise
C. difficulties that cannot be prevented by the supervisor cannot be overcome
D. the solution of problems in supervision is best achieved by scientific methods

10. Suppose that a stenographer recently appointed to your bureau submits a memorandum suggesting a change in office procedure that has been tried before and has been found unsuccessful. 10.____
Of the following, the BEST action for you to take is to
A. send the stenographer a note acknowledging receipt of the suggestion, but do not attempt to carry out the suggestion
B. point out that suggestions should come from her supervisor, who has a better knowledge of the problems of the office
C. try out the suggested change a second time, lest the stenographer lose interest in her work
D. call the stenographer in, explain the change is not practicable, and compliment her for her interest and alertness

11. Suppose that you are an assistant to one of the important administrators in your department. You receive a note from the head of the department asking your superior to assist with a pressing problem that has arisen by making an immediate recommendation. Your superior is out of town on official business for a few days and cannot be reached. The head of the department, evidently, is not aware of his absence. 11.____
Of the following, the BEST action for you to take is
   A. send the note back to the head of the department without comment so as not to incriminate your supervisor
   B. forward the note to one of the administrators in another division of the department
   C. wait until your supervisor returns and bring the note to his attention immediately
   D. get in touch with the head of the department immediately and inform him that your superior is out of town

12. One of your duties may be to estimate the budget of your unit for the next fiscal year. Suppose that you expect no important changes in the work of your unit during the next year. 12.____
Of the following, the MOST appropriate basis for estimating next year's budget is the
   A. average budget of your unit for the last five years
   B. budget of your unit for the current year plus fifty percent to allow for possible expansion
   C. average current budget of units in your department
   D. budget of your unit for the current fiscal year

13. Suppose that you are acting as supervisor to an important administrator in your department. Of the following, the BEST reason for keeping a separate *pending* file of letters to which answers are expected very soon is that 13.____
   A. important correspondence should be placed in a separate, readily accessible file
   B. a periodic check of the *pending* file will indicate the possible need for follow-up letters
   C. correspondence is never final, so provision should be made for keeping files open
   D. there is seldom sufficient room in the permanent files to permit filing all letters

14. In order to BEST able to teach a newly appointed employee who must learn to do a type of work which is unfamiliar to him, his supervisor should realize that during the first stage in the learning process the subordinate is generally characterized by 14.____
   A. acute consciousness of self
   B. acute consciousness of subject matter, with little interest in persons or personalities
   C. inertness or passive acceptance of assigned role
   D. understanding of problems without understanding of the means of solving them

15. The MOST accurate of the following principles of education and learning for a supervisor to keep in mind when planning a training program for the employees under his supervision is that 15.____
    A. his employees, like all other individuals, vary in the rate at which they learn new material and in the degree to which they can retain what they do learn
    B. experienced employees who have the same basic college education and agency experience will be able to learn new material at approximately the same rate of speed
    C. the speed with which employees can learn new material after the age of forty is half as rapid as at ages twenty to thirty
    D. with regard to any specific task, it is easier and takes less time to break an experienced employee of old, unsatisfactory work habits than it is to teach him new, acceptable ones

16. A supervisor has been transferred from supervision of one group of units to another group of units in the same center. He spends the first three weeks in his new assignment in getting acquainted with his new subordinates, their caseload problems, and their work. In this process, he notices that some of the case records and forms which are submitted to him by two of the assistant supervisors are carelessly or improperly prepared. 16.____
    The BEST of the following actions for the supervisor to take in this situation is to
    A. carefully check the work submitted by these assistant supervisors during an additional three weeks before taking any more positive action
    B. confer with these offending workers and show each one where his work needs improvement and how to go about achieving it
    C. institute an in-service training program specifically designed to solve such a problem and instruct the entire subordinate staff in proper work methods
    D. make a note of these errors for documentary use in preparing the annual service rating reports and advise the workers involved to prepare their work more carefully

17. A supervisor, who was promoted to his position a year ago, has supervised a certain assistant supervisor for this one year. The work of the assistant supervisor has been very poor because he has done a minimum of work, refused to take sufficient responsibility, been difficult to handle, and required very close supervision. Apparently, due to the increasing insistency by his supervisor that he improve the caliber of his work, he assistant supervisor tenders his resignation, stating that the demands of the job are too much for him. The opinion of the previous supervisor, who had supervised this assistant supervisor for two years, agrees substantially with that of the new supervisor. 17.____
    Under such circumstances, the BEST of the following actions the supervisor can take in general is to
    A. recommend that the resignation be accepted and that he be rehired should he later apply when he feels able to do the job
    B. recommend that the resignation be accepted and that he not be rehired should he later so apply

C. refuse to accept the resignation but try to persuade the assistant supervisor to accept psychiatric help
D. refuse to accept the resignation, promising the assistant supervisor that he will be less closely supervised in the future since he is now so experienced

18. Rumors have arisen to the effect that one of the social investigators under your supervision has been attending classes at a local university during afternoon hours when he is supposed to be making field visits. 18.____
The BEST of the following ways for you to approach this problem is to
A. disregard the rumors since, like most rumors, they probably have no actual foundation in fact
B. have a discreet investigation made in order to determine the actual facts prior to taking any other action
C. inform the investigator that you know what he has been doing and that such behavior is overt dereliction of duty and is punishable by dismissal
D. review the investigator's work record, spot check his cases and take no further action unless the quality of his work is below average for the unit

19. The one of the following instances when it is MOST important for an upper level supervisor to follow the chain of command is when he is 19.____
A. communicating decisions
B. communicating information
C. receiving suggestions
D. seeking information

20. In order to maintain a proper relationship with a worker who is assigned to staff rather than line functions, a line supervisor should 20.____
A. accept all recommendations of the staff worker
B. include the staff worker in the conferences called by the supervisor for his subordinates
C. keep the staff worker informed of developments in the area of his staff assignment
D. require that the staff worker's recommendations be communicated to the supervisor through the supervisor's own superior

21. Of the following, the GREATEST disadvantage of placing a worker in a staff position under the direct supervision of the supervisor whom he advises is the possibility that the 21.____
A. staff worker will tend to be insubordinate because of a feeling of superiority over the supervisor
B. staff worker will tend to give advice of the type which the supervisor wants to hear or finds acceptable
C. supervisor will tend to be mistrustful of the advice of a worker of subordinate rank
D. supervisor will tend to derive little benefit from the advice because to supervise properly he should know at least as much as his subordinate

22. One factor which might be given consideration in deciding upon the optimum span of control of a supervisor over his immediate subordinates is the position of the supervisor in the hierarchy of the organization. It is generally considered PROPER that the number of subordinates immediately supervised by a higher, upper echelon supervisor 22.____
    A. is unrelated to and tends to form no pattern with the number supervised by lower level supervisors
    B. should be about the same as the number supervised by a lower level supervisor
    C. should be larger than the number supervised by a lower level supervisor
    D. should be smaller than the number supervised by a lower level supervisor

23. An important administrative problem is how precisely to define the limits on authority that are delegated to subordinate supervisors. Such definition of limits of authority should be 23.____
    A. as precise as possible and practicable in all areas
    B. as precise as possible and practicable in areas of function, but should allow considerable flexibility in the area of personnel management
    C. as precise as possible and practicable in the area of personnel management, but should allow considerable flexibility both in the areas of function and in the areas of personnel management
    D. in general terms so as to allow considerable flexibility both in the areas of function and in the areas of personnel management

24. The one of the following causes of clerical error which is usually considered to be LEAST attributable to faulty supervision or inefficient management is 24.____
    A. inability to carry out instructions
    B. too much work to do
    C. an inappropriate record-keeping system
    D. continual interruptions

25. Assume that you are the supervisor of a clerical unit in a large agency. One of your subordinates violates a rule of the agency, a violation which requires that the employee be suspended from his work for one day. The violated rule is one that you have found to be unduly strict and you have recommended to the management of the agency that the rule be changed or abolished. The management has been considering your recommendation but has not yet reached a decision on the matter. 25.____
    In these circumstances, you should
    A. not initiate disciplinary action, but, instead, explain to the employee that the rule may be changed shortly
    B. delay disciplinary action on the violation until the management has reached a decision on changing the rule
    C. modify the disciplinary action by reprimanding the employee and informing him that further action may be taken when the management has reached a decision on changing the rule
    D. initiate the prescribed disciplinary action without commenting on the strictness of the rule or on your recommendation

KEY (CORRECT ANSWERS)

1.	C	11.	D
2.	C	12.	D
3.	D	13.	B
4.	A	14.	A
5.	C	15.	A
6.	C	16.	B
7.	C	17.	B
8.	B	18.	B
9.	B	19.	A
10.	D	20.	C

21.	B
22.	D
23.	A
24.	A
25.	D

TEST 2

DIRECTIONS: Each question or incomplete statement is followed by several suggested answers or completions. Select the one that BEST answers the question or completes the statement. *PRINT THE LETTER OF THE CORRECT ANSWER IN THE SPACE AT THE RIGHT.*

1. As a supervisor, assume that a newly appointed employee is assigned to your unit. 1.____
The one of the following which is likely to have the LEAST value in motivating the new employee when he first reports to you is
   A. an explanation of disciplinary measures which may be taken against employees
   B. indication by you that he can always come to you for help
   C. the first impression he gets of you and his fellow employees
   D. your emphasis on the importance of the work when interviewing him

2. Assume that you are in charge of a unit of employees. A new appointee reports to you for the first time. 2.____
Of the following, the MOST advisable action for you to take first is to
   A. attempt to evaluate his attitude towards the work he will be required to perform
   B. discuss with him the general nature of the duties he is to perform
   C. explain the opportunities he will have for promotion within the department
   D. have him read over any available material pertaining to departmental rules and regulations for employees

3. Your department conducts a formal training course for new appointees. 3.____
Under these circumstances, a supervisor should assume that
   A. he can safely delegate all responsibility for any additional training required to one of his experienced men who will work with the new appointee in the field
   B. he is thus relieved of the effort required to train new appointees who may be assigned to his unit
   C. he will still be responsible for supplementary training of new appointees assigned to his unit
   D. his responsibility for training should be limited to making suggestions for improving the formal training program based on his observation of the work of new appointees

4. In the development of an on-the-job training program, the FIRST step should be 4.____
   A. consideration of the cost of such a program
   B. consideration of the problem of interesting the workers in such a program
   C. determination of the training facilities which may be available
   D. determination of those areas in which training is required

5. Assume that a recent appointee has completed whatever basic training was provided for him. It becomes necessary to give him a special assignment for which he has not been specifically trained. He is given this assignment without any instructions as to how it should be carried out. This should be considered as 5.____
   A. *advisable*, because a worker has to feel his own way on special assignments
   B. *advisable*, because there comes a time when a worker should be encouraged to exercise his own initiative
   C. *inadvisable*, because a worker needs guidance on any aspect of the job with which he is unfamiliar
   D. *inadvisable*, because various superior officials of the department may have different ideas concerning the methods to be used in special assignments

6. Assume that you are holding a conference with the works in your unit. During the conference, one of the employees, in an offensive manner, challenges a statement you make. You are reasonably sure but not certain that what you have said is correct. 6.____
   The MOST advisable action for you to take at the conference is to
   A. admit that you may be in error but reprimand the man for his manner of speaking
   B. avail yourself of the opportunity to point out to the group what constitutes bad manners
   C. ignore the man's manner but make sure that the group feels your statement is correct
   D. say that you will determine the correct facts as soon as possible and inform the staff

7. Suppose that a new inspectional procedure has been ordered by the chief of your bureau. You think that it may meet with some objection by your staff. 7.____
   As a unit supervisor, the MOST advisable action for you to take in order to minimize such resistance is to
   A. appoint a committee from your staff to study the procedure and report on its advantages and disadvantages
   B. discuss, at a staff conference, the intent of the new procedure and the means of carrying it out
   C. inform the staff that this is an order coming from a higher authority and it must be carried out regardless of personal feelings
   D. issue detailed instructions concerning the new procedure to each member of your staff

8. Suppose that at conferences with your staff, you find that, usually, only one of the men participates in the discussion. 8.____
   Under these circumstances, the MOST advisable action for you to take is to
   A. speak to him privately and ask him to refrain from speaking so much at staff conferences
   B. stimulate the other men by asking them direct questions at staff conferences

C. tell him directly, at conferences, that you would prefer to hear from the other men for a change
D. use the technique of not looking at this man when asking questions in order to prevent him from getting the floor

9. Which of the following do you consider to be the MOST important factor to be considered in evaluating the work of an employee. His 9.____
A. ability to maintain good personal relationships with his supervisor, his fellow workers, and the community
B. effectiveness in helping to carry out the objectives of the program
C. observance of departmental rules and regulations governing employees
D. personal awareness of the significance of his work to the welfare of the community

10. Of the following, the MOST valid statement concerning the supervisor and the probationary period is: 10.____
A. Proper personnel selection methods should make it unnecessary for supervisory personnel to be concerned with evaluation of probationers
B. Requiring an immediate supervisor to report on the capability of a candidate at the end of his probationary period is inadvisable since he usually has had no part in the initial selection of personnel
C. The probationary period should be considered as an integral part of the personnel selection process and, thus, should be an active concern of immediate supervisors
D. The value of a probationary period is likely to be greater when the supervisor is required to report only when he considers a candidate not suitable for permanent appointment rather when he is required to certify that a candidate is suitable

11. An employee under your supervision complains to you about the fact that you recommended him for a performance rating indicating merely satisfactory work. He feels that he deserves a higher rating, while you are convinced that your recommendation was justified. 11.____
Of the following, the MOST advisable action for you to take is to
A. advise him of his right to appeal the rating given and the required procedure for making such an appeal
B. explain to him that, as a supervisor, your experience and your opportunity to evaluate his work against that of other employees enable you to give him a fair and just rating
C. give him your specific reasons for considering his performance average or satisfactory and not qualifying for a higher rating
D. point out to him that relatively few persons receive an above-average rating and that there is always opportunity for a higher rating in the future

12. Assume that your superior has assigned to your unit a special investigation which is to be completed by a certain date. Considering the regular work load, you feel that the investigation cannot be completed in the allotted time. You point this out to him but he insists that you handle the assignment without any increase in staff. 12.____
Of the following, the MOST advisable course of action for you to take is to
    A. agree to undertake the assignment but insist upon some assurance that this situation will not be repeated
    B. be as noncommittal as possible with the determination to secure evidence to show that you should not be given the assignment
    C. take the matter up with higher authority but inform him that you have done so
    D. undertake the assignment with the intention to keep him closely informed concerning the progress of the work

13. Assume that, as a supervisor, you have received somewhat conflicting orders from two superiors not of equal rank. 13.____
Of the following, the MOST advisable course of action for you to follow is to
    A. attempt to carry out the orders of each superior as far as you can
    B. carry out the orders of the person higher in rank
    C. consult your immediate superior concerning the situation
    D. use your own judgment and follow those orders which seem more reasonable

14. Assume that you are a supervisor. Your immediate superior frequently gives assignments to your subordinates without your knowledge. 14.____
Of the following, the MOST advisable way for you to handle this situation is to
    A. discuss it with your immediate supervisor
    B. instruct your staff that they are to accept assignments only from you
    C. keep a record of such instances and forward a memorandum concerning them to higher authority in the department
    D. realize and accept the fact that, as your superior, he has authority over you

15. Of the following, the one which would LEAST likely aid a supervisor in long-range planning is 15.____
    A. a practical attitude of not worrying about possible problems until they arise
    B. estimating future needs on the basis of past experience
    C. obtaining early knowledge of contemplated changes
    D. staff conferences with the employees under his supervision

16. Of the following, the one that is likely to be of LEAST value as a direct source of help for a supervisor is 16.____
    A. a compilation of departmental rules and regulations
    B. a manual of standard operating procedures
    C. civil service rules and regulations
    D. the personnel officer of the department

17. Assume that you suspect that a field worker under your supervision goes home early in the afternoon. In spotchecking one of his daily reports, you find that he has indicated that his last inspection was made at a certain establishment at 4 P.M. The owner of the establishment states that the inspection was made at 1 P.M. 17.____
Of the following, the MOST advisable course of action for you to take FIRST is to
   A. attempt to determine whether any animosity exists between the owner of this establishment and the employee
   B. check with owners of establishments listed on the report as having been visited before the establishment in question was visited
   C. confront the employee with the information you have obtained from the owner of the establishment
   D. send a report of these circumstances to your immediate supervisor

18. Assume that one of the employees under your supervision is frequently absent. Although you have discussed the matter with him several times, his attendance record remains unsatisfactory. 18.____
The MOST advisable course of action for you to take NEXT is to
   A. discuss the problem again with the employee to see if any new factors have arisen which cause his continued absence
   B. give him another chance
   C. recommend that appropriate penalties be applied since the problem has already been discussed with him
   D. advise him to seek expert counsel concerning his personal problems

19. Assume that you are a supervisor. One of the men you supervise angrily demands an interview with you to discuss his dissatisfaction with his work assignment. 19.____
Of the following, the course of action you should take FIRST in this situation is to
   A. advise him to take the matter up with your superior
   B. arrange for a private interview as soon as possible to discuss his grievance
   C. explain to the employee that all assignments are made by you only after consideration of what is best for satisfactory accomplishment of the work of the unit
   D. promise the employee that you will review the work assignments in your unit to determine whether any changes are warranted

20. Of the following, the one which would likely aid a supervisor MOST in maintaining morale among his staff is 20.____
   A. ignoring any rumors that are transmitted through the organization's grapevine
   B. maintenance of an aloof attitude in his contacts with the group under his supervision

C. scrupulous care in not revealing any information which the administration requests him to treat as confidential
D. seeking, through consultation with his own superior, to find a remedy if situations outside of his division threaten to upset his own group

21. Of the following, the one which a supervisor should try to avoid MOST is 21.____
A. consideration that rumors in the organization may contain some elements of truth
B. handling of grievances which are voiced by his entire staff, as opposed to individual grievances
C. offering personal counsel when it is requested of him by subordinates
D. use of disciplinary measures to secure proper conduct of subordinates

22. Suppose that you are a supervisor. At a social function which you attend, unfavorable remarks concerning certain activities of our department are made in the course of conversation. You happen to be in agreement with what is being said. 22.____
Under these circumstances, you should consider that
A. it is best to be noncommittal in such situations
B. it is necessary for you to convince the others of the value of these activities
C. it would be advisable for you to suggest that those interested write a group letter of complaint to the department
D. you are a private citizen as well as a public employee and, therefore, are free to express your personal opinion at a social function

23. Assume that you are a supervisor in charge of an inspectional unit. A merchant whose weighing and measuring devices were tested by one of the inspectors under your supervision takes the trouble to write a letter of complaint to the Commissioner of the department. In this letter he states that the manner in which the inspection was conducted gave customers in the store the impression that improper devices were being used although no violations were found. The letter is referred to you for appropriate action. 23.____
Of the following, the MOST advisable action for you to take FIRST is to
A. arrange for an inspector not known by the accused inspector to observe him in the field and report his findings to you
B. call a staff meeting at which you will discuss proper procedures to be used when making inspections
C. interview the inspector involved to get his version of the incident
D. make personal observations, in the field, of the manner in which inspections are being conducted

24. In attempting to protect consumers against various types of fraud, the law states that, in certain instances, possession of a certain substance by a dealer is presumptive evidence of his intent to use it to defraud. 24.____
From the point of view of the enforcing agency, the PRINCIPAL value of such legislation is that
A. it offers more protection of the rights of the consumer than it does of the rights of the dealer
rights of the dealer

B. such evidence, by its very nature, is superior to direct evidence
C. the agency is relieved of the difficulties involved in attempting to obtain direct evidence
D. this constitutes a more comprehensive definition of the offense involved

25. Departments of municipal government frequently suggest the enactment of legislation in fields in which they are interested. 25.____
Such suggestions are
A. *advisable*, because basic legislation is already available
B. *advisable*, because the departments have the best knowledge of their problems and needs
C. *inadvisable*, because the city already has a Law Department
D. *inadvisable*, because departments have biased viewpoints

KEY (CORRECT ANSWERS)

1. A
2. B
3. C
4. D
5. C

6. D
7. B
8. B
9. B
10. C

11. C
12. D
13. C
14. A
15. A

16. C
17. B
18. C
19. B
20. D

21. D
22. A
23. C
24. C
25. B

KEY (CORRECT ANSWERS)

EXAMINATION SECTION
TEST 1

DIRECTIONS: Each question or incomplete statement is followed by several suggested answers or completions. Select the one that BEST answers the question or completes the statement. *PRINT THE LETTER OF THE CORRECT ANSWER IN THE SPACE AT THE RIGHT.*

1. Ms. Palmer is a manager who has the reputation of being tough, but fair-minded. She has just been promoted into a different part of the agency, and now heads a unit of thirty employees. She has observed that there are several employees who stick together. They seem to really enjoy working together, and she has observed them discussing how to solve work problems even on their lunch breaks. While she realizes they are effective and good at what they do, she does not like the idea of this informal work group staying together and possibly becoming more powerful and a threat to her authority. She decides to take steps to weaken its effectiveness. 1.____
The proposed action of Ms. Palmer is a

   A. *good* idea, since supervisors need complete control of their units
   B. *bad* idea, since the employees are having a good time and not causing trouble
   C. *good* idea, since the informal work group is most likely seen as a clique and resented by other employees
   D. *bad* idea, since the informal work group is functioning effectively, and she is most likely reacting in a defensive manner

2. The middle manager is both *player* and *coach* and needs to combine different skills and actions. A middle manager must see the *big picture,* be detached, and have a more long-range perspective. But he or she also needs to have detailed knowledge of the job, abundant job experience, and the ability to become deeply involved in the work. 2.____
It is sometimes difficult for a middle manager to know if he or she is employing the correct blend of these roles. Is he or she too involved in being a player—doing too many things that should be done by others? Or is he or she being too much of a coach—delegating too much and not being involved enough? How much one needs to be player or coach is unique to every situation and very much influenced, not only by the actual job to be done, but also by the needs and demands of bosses, co-workers, and employees.
With which of the following choices would the author MOST likely agree?

   A. When in doubt, a middle manager is likely to be better off delegating an assignment.
   B. If a middle manager has very competent employees, he or she is likely to be better off being a *player* than a *coach.*
   C. If a middle manager has a very demanding boss, he or she is likely to be better off being a *player.*
   D. If a situation calls for technical information that only the middle manager has, he or she is likely to be better off being a *player.*

3. Bob supervises fifteen employees in Unit 2, a position he has held for nine months. Before being promoted, he had worked in the same unit for four years and was well liked by all of his co-workers. He was an excellent employee and worked very hard. Bob has had a number of problems since receiving his promotion, however. A new employee in his unit seems to have an aversion to work. He frequently comes in late and makes many personal phone calls during the day. Bob has noticed this behavior, but is reluctant to do anything about it. Because he is not sure if the work he assigns the employee will get done, he gives much less work to him than to the others. Since the unit has a higher workload than ever, the work is piling up, and everyone in the unit is concerned. 3.____
One day, one of the personnel managers approaches Bob, tells him that the employees in the unit are upset about the situation, and urges him to take action. The next day, Bob calls a meeting of the staff and announces that *some people in the unit are coming in late, spending too much time on the phone, and not getting any work done.* He also says that this has to stop. That afternoon, Bob sends everyone in his unit a memo which emphasizes these points and bans any future personal calls in the office.
Bob's way of handling this situation was

   A. *wise,* since this should have the effect of *shaping up* the other workers in the unit as well
   B. *unwise,* since it will lower productivity
   C. *unwise,* since it is too indirect and punitive a response
   D. *wise,* since he would have hurt the new employee's feelings if he had confronted him alone

4. You supervise a large unit of thirty employees. Diane, an employee in the unit, comes to you and says she can't work for Alan, her supervisor, anymore because he checks on her work all the time and is very critical of her. 4.____
She says she has tried to talk to him about the situation, but he won't listen to her.
Of the following, it would be BEST if you responded by saying

   A. *"I'm sure Alan is treating you no differently than he treats everyone else"*
   B. *"Do you feel Alan is too critical of you?"*
   C. *"I don't think you should have gone over Alan's head by coming to me with this minor problem."*
   D. *"You wouldn't want Alan to accept poor quality work, would you?"*

5. Which of the following statements is MOST accurate? 5.____

   A. It is much better for supervisors to focus on an employee's behavior rather than on his or her personality.
   B. It is not common for supervisors to procrastinate, hoping a problem will go away.
   C. Problems in working habits are always more difficult for supervisors to deal with than performance problems.
   D. When discussing an employee's behavior, it is wise for a supervisor to attribute motives to the behavior.

6. All of the following are likely to be true of a new supervisory situation EXCEPT: 6.____

   A. New supervisors are often on the spot during their first few weeks on the job
   B. Some new supervisors swell with responsibility instead of growing with it
   C. It is best if a new supervisor begins by making a lot of changes
   D. Former cronies of the new supervisor may expect special treatment and become resentful if it is not given

7. You have been the supervisor of a small unit for four months. One of the employees you supervise has consistently performed very poorly. You have talked with her on many occasions and evaluated her performance and set goals regularly. None of this has helped, although she does have the necessary skills to do the job. It seems that she just does not like to work very hard. She has been employed by the organization for thirty years, and other long-time employees have told you she has always performed poorly, but her other supervisors always overlooked her poor performance because they knew she would make a lot of trouble if she were formally disciplined. Your unit's workload has increased significantly in the past three months, and now the other employees must do a great deal of the work she is unwilling to do. 7.____
   Of the following, which would be the BEST action for you to take?

   A. Discuss the situation with the employee and tell her you will have to begin formal discipline procedures if her performance does not improve.
   B. Ask the employee to resign.
   C. Ask one of the long-time employees to discuss the situation with her, encouraging her to resign.
   D. Ask your supervisor to fire her.

8. An employee you supervise is extremely competitive and very abrasive. The other employees in your unit are very resentful of this employee, who often *shows them up* with the very high quality of his work. 8.____
   Of the following, it would be BEST if you

   A. let him know that, while you appreciate his concern and attempts to produce high quality work, the ability to get along with others and work as a team is just as important as technical ability
   B. ignore the situation, since his work is of such high quality
   C. let him know that, although you appreciate the high quality of his work, you can't help but get irritated by some of his behavior
   D. try to understand why he is acting the way he is

9. You have the responsibility of making a big decision, and you would like to get some group input. 9.____
   Of the following, it is MOST important that you

   A. make sure everyone in the group has a chance to speak
   B. make it clear whether you will abide by their suggestions, or whether you just want to hear these suggestions to help you arrive at a possible solution
   C. wait until everyone has spoken before silently deciding whether to consider their ideas
   D. use good problem-solving techniques during the meeting

10. Which of the following statements is LEAST accurate? 10.____

A. Most workers want to satisfy physical, social, and personal needs.
B. A supervisor can have a significant impact upon an employee's personal life.
C. Supervisors who emphasize getting to know the needs of their employees are not using their time wisely.
D. Most workers want responsibilities they can handle, results they can demonstrate, and recognition for what they accomplish.

11. You are the supervisor of a unit of twenty employees. Janet, one of the employees, comes to you and says that Mark, her supervisor, is not supervising. She says he does not take the time to give her direction or feedback on her work. Janet also says that she often has had to do assignments that should have been handled by Mark. Janet understands that Mark has a large workload, but says that she does too. She has tried to talk to Mark several times about the situation, but says he won't acknowledge that there is a problem. Both Janet and Mark have performed well in the past. 11.____
How would you handle this situation?

A. Inform Janet that she should not have ignored the chain of command by going over Mark's head.
B. Ask Janet to be more understanding of the pressures faced by Mark.
C. Thank Janet for coming to you, but explain that there is nothing you can do.
D. Discuss the situation with Mark.

12. It is now widely recognized that salaries, benefits, and working conditions have more of an impact on job satisfaction than on motivation. If they are not satisfactory, work performance and morale will suffer. But even when they are very good, employees will not necessarily be motivated to work well. For example, The Wall Street Journal recently reported that as many as 40% or 50% of newly hired Wall Street lawyers (whose salaries start at upwards of $90,000) quit within the first three years, citing long hours, pressures, and monotony as the prime offenders. It seems there is just not enough of an intellectual challenge in their jobs. An up-and-coming money-market executive concluded: *Whether it was $1 million or $100 million, the procedure was the same. Except for the tension, a baboon could have done my job.* When money and benefits are adequate, the most important additional determinants of job satisfaction are more responsibility, a sense of achievement, recognition, and a chance to advance. And all of these have a more significant influence on employee motivation and performance. 12.____
If you were a supervisor who agreed with the above passage, which of the following would you MOST likely do?

A. Press hard for large monetary bonuses for well-paid executives that you supervise
B. Encourage employee involvement in establishing employee assistance programs
C. Encourage employee participation in job design and decision-making
D. Encourage *Employee of the Year* awards

13. A supervisor feels very comfortable with two of the employees she supervises because they have work styles very similar to her own. 13.____
Of the following, the supervisor should

A. feel confident that the employees are doing a very good job
B. try to view their work as subjectively as possible
C. try to view their work as objectively as possible
D. carefully reevaluate their past work performance

14. Nelson is a perfectionist who often becomes overwhelmed because he is trying to do too much too well. He has extremely high expectations and seems to be showing signs of *burnout*. Nelson just cannot say no—he will take on anything, even if someone else could or should do it. And nothing leaves his desk unless it is done perfectly. You know he is taking a lot of work home with him in order to keep up. 14.____
Assume that you are Nelson's supervisor.
Which of the following do you feel would be the BEST way to handle the above situation?

A. Enroll Nelson in a course on assertiveness.
B. Discuss with Nelson the issues of working too hard and trying to be perfect and the consequences of these.
C. Sit down with Nelson and let him know it is all right to make mistakes.
D. Enroll Nelson in a course on establishing priorities.

15. Which of the following statements is LEAST accurate? 15.____

A. In order to be highly productive, it usually does not matter whether a work group feels the general organizational climate is a fair and friendly one.
B. Work groups are likely to contain an informal alignment based on status and authority.
C. Supervisors should accept the subgroups that often form within work units.
D. It is not desirable for a supervisor to be seen as an outsider imposing controls on members of the work group.

16. When conducting a corrective interview, a supervisor should do all of the following EXCEPT 16.____

A. state the purpose of the interview
B. change the employee's point of view
C. state the problem, review expectations, and review the employee's current performance
D. give time frames

17. Derogatory criticism of a person's work can be very harmful. A supervisor should be able to correct an employee without destroying his or her self-worth. A very minor example is a typist's mistake or typographical error that is sent back along with a 3x5 sheet of paper on which the typist's name is written, underlined, and deliberately misspelled. To me and the other typists in my department, it is a little degrading and implies a certain amount of ignorance and a lack of respect. Little things add up to a lot. 17.____
Which of the following statements is BEST supported by the above passage?

A. Respect and dignity on the job are important to employees.
B. Supervisors should only criticize an employee's work when they absolutely have to.
C. A supervisor's ability to take criticism well is important in order to set an example for the supervisor's employees.
D. Give employees an inch and they'll take a mile.

18. You have just received a promotion to a different unit. Until he failed the oral exam for the title, Murray, a long-time and well-liked employee, had briefly held this position provisionally. You have been in the job for two weeks and have noticed that Murray is very bitter about the situation and is subtly undermining your authority. Of the following, it would be BEST if you 18.___

A. had Murray transferred as soon as possible
B. spoke with Murray about the situation
C. spoke with your supervisor about the situation and asked him or her to talk with the employee
D. ignored the situation for two more weeks to give Murray more time to adjust to it

19. *I believe that many of the problems I encountered were problems of fit with the informal organization. My peers and supervisors were unable to perceive me as being able to perform the job that the company hired me for. Their reaction to me was disbelief. I was out of the "place" normally filled by black people in the company; and since no black person had preceded me successfully, it was easy for my antagonists to believe I was inadequate, and to act as if I were.* 19.___

– A black manager on his experience in the early 1960's

Which of the following statements is BEST supported by the above passage?

A. The informal organization is often beyond a supervisor's best efforts to control it.
B. Expectations can significantly affect behavior and perceptions.
C. Informal organizations wield little power.
D. Informal organizations are very powerful.

20. You supervise a unit of twenty employees. Sometimes you must ask your employees to work overtime. You are careful to allocate the overtime fairly. Most of the employees are cooperative, but Andy always resists. Tonight he said that you deliberately pick him to work on Monday nights because you are afraid to ask anyone else to miss the football game on TV. 20.___

Of the following, it would be BEST if you responded by saying:

A. *"It's your own fault for always resisting overtime."*
B. *"If you think you aren't getting a fair deal on over time, we can discuss it, but I do need you to work overtime tonight."*
C. *"It's only a game. Besides, I've been fairly allocating overtime on Monday nights to every employee on a regular schedule."*
D. *"I really don't think I've been singling you out."*

21. When supervising, it is BEST for supervisors to 21.____

A. focus primarily on appearances
B. refine their hidden expectations
C. focus on an employee's attitude toward the job as a basis for performance evaluation
D. know the job standards and be sure employees know them too

22. You are the manager of a large unit of fifty employees. Jane, a typist in the unit, comes to you with a complaint about her supervisor, Marie. Marie is a program analyst who transferred to your unit last year. Jane, a very good and reliable worker, tells you that Marie has been taking up a lot of the secretaries' and other workers' time by talking with them a great deal about projects she is working on. Jane says she realizes that Marie is insecure about her work and needs a lot of support, but her behavior is causing some disruption. Because you are Marie's supervisor, she asks you to intervene. 22.____
Of the following choices, it would be BEST if you

A. went over Marie's personnel records for clues of poor performance and then discuss the situation with her
B. told Jane she should have gone directly to Marie to discuss the problem, instead of coming to you
C. asked Jane for more proof
D. called Marie in to ask her how she is doing, and asked if you could do anything to make her feel more comfortable on the job

23. Of the following statements, which would MOST likely be appropriate for a supervisor to say to someone he or she supervises? 23.____

A. *"I'm concerned about the impact your long coffee breaks are having on the other employees. I'd like you to shorten them."*
B. *"Time off next week? You must be kidding!"*
C. *"You must be pretty thirsty to take all those long coffee breaks."*
D. *"I get annoyed every time I see you coming in late."*

24. When Napoleon was asked why he reinstituted the symbolic and practically worthless Legion of Honor Medal, he replied, *you lead men by baubles, not words.* 24.____
Another way to say that would be that a supervisor

A. gives all of the employees she supervises *outstanding* evaluations
B. never overly praises those he supervises
C. passes out trophies annually to outstanding employees
D. praises those she supervises only when they deserve it

25. All of the following are common problems faced by new supervisors EXCEPT 25.____

A. difficulty in making decisions because of the fear of making a mistake
B. spending too much time procrastinating or collecting data before making a decision
C. success in delegating work
D. succumbing to waves of inertia because of fear

KEY (CORRECT ANSWERS)

1.	D	11.	D
2.	D	12.	C
3.	C	13.	C
4.	B	14.	B
5.	A	15.	A
6.	C	16.	B
7.	A	17.	A
8.	A	18.	B
9.	B	19.	B
10.	C	20.	B

21.	D
22.	A
23.	A
24.	C
25.	C

8. *Our control systems are designed under the apparent assumption that ninety percent of the people are lazy ne'er-do-wells, just waiting to lie, cheat, steal.... We demoralize the ninety-five percent of the workforce who do act like adults by designing systems to cover our tails against the five percent who are bad actors.* 8.____
A supervisor who believed the above statement would MOST likely

   A. give employees more discretion in performing tasks
   B. supervise employees very closely
   C. supervise problem employees more loosely than other supervisors would
   D. give employees less discretion in performing tasks

9. All of the following are common problems found in new supervisors EXCEPT 9.____

   A. an over- or underestimation of what they can accomplish
   B. an unwillingness to accept positive feedback from those they supervise
   C. overly flattering behavior towards their supervisors
   D. a tendency to become overly concerned with appearance rather than substance

10. Phyllis is a typist who works in a small typing pool. She has worked there for a year and a half, and has received excellent evaluations. Phyllis is a 24-year-old white female. Her supervisor is Patricia, a 45-year-old white female. They have always gotten along well, and morale in the unit is good. There are five white females and one Hispanic female in the unit. 10.____
One night, Phyllis and her husband, who is black, ran into Patricia and her husband as they were leaving the movie theater. Phyllis noticed that Patricia seemed uncomfortable, but didn't think much more about it. The following Monday, Patricia asked Phyllis how she enjoyed the movie. She also asked if that was Phyllis' husband with her. When Phyllis replied that it was, Patricia gave her a weak smile, talked a little more, and left. Since that time, Patricia has been quite cold to Phyllis. For the last month, Phyllis has noticed that she has been getting all of the assignments for typing tabular material and other difficult typing that no one else wants. Previously, this work had been evenly distributed among all of the typists.
The above passage is an example of

   A. comparable worth
   B. subtle discrimination
   C. sexual harassment
   D. equal pay for equal work

11. At a staff meeting, another supervisor made a comment that you felt was very critical of your department. You are about to meet with him in his office. 11.____
Of the following, it would be BEST if you said,

   A. *"I really didn't appreciate that comment you made about my department during the staff meeting."*
   B. *"That sure was an interesting staff meeting. I learned a lot. How about you?"*
   C. *"I was concerned about your comments on my department this morning. Do you have any suggestions on how I might improve things?"*
   D. *"I was interested in what you had to say today in the staff meeting. I feel some of your remarks were critical of my department, and I'd like to talk with you about them."*

12. Donna's style has no doubt increased her supervisor's risk of heart attack significantly. She is a procrastinator and a last minute operator. She seems to thrive on the challenge of these self-imposed tight deadlines. Her supervisor has even tried lying and pushing the deadline of a project up a week before it was really due, but somehow she always finds out the truth. The quality of her work is excellent, but her supervisor never can be sure a project will be finished on time. Her supervisor feels he could not constantly work under that sort of stress and cannot imagine that Donna is not going to succumb to the pressure one of these days and miss a deadline. Besides, he feels all that stress is not good for her health. 12.___
The BEST way to handle the above situation is for Donna's superior to

A. do nothing
B. call her in to his office and lecture her about the importance of not procrastinating
C. anonymously send her a book on planning and time management
D. threaten her with severe formal disciplinary action unless she stops procrastinating

13. Barbara is an employee who has a reputation for being a troublemaker. She comes to her supervisor, Jack Burns, and says she is being sexually harassed. Barbara accuses Jack's superior, David London, who has been a close friend of Jack's for many years. Jack should 13.___

A. take Barbara's complaint seriously
B. refer Barbara to counseling or to an employee assistance program
C. listen to Barbara sympathetically, advise her to go to the affirmative action office to file a complaint, but also warn David that a complaint is going to be filed against him
D. ask Barbara if she has any documentation to support her allegations

14. Which of the following statements about supervision is LEAST accurate? 14.___

A. Once an employee performs well, he or she will continue to perform at that level.
B. It is important for supervisors to encourage the employees they supervise to employ good delegation skills.
C. Hidden expectations a supervisor may have, like assuming an employee does not mind taking work home, can be harmful.
D. Supervisors should always be trying to improve their supervisory skills.

15. Which of the following would NOT be considered an example of subtle discrimination against an employee who is a protected class member? 15.___
A superior

A. protects a protected class member by never giving negative feedback and by giving easy assignments
B. asks a highly respected protected class member in the unit to talk with a Hispanic employee about a performance problem
C. treats black male employees with more respect than she treats white male employees
D. shares important information much more with male employees than with female employees

16. You supervise eight employees. In order to protect all of them from eyestrain, one particular assignment that requires close eyework is rotated and shared by everyone. One of the employees has just complained to you that he receives more of this work than the others, and he wants to be excused from doing the work today. You are not completely sure that he is incorrect. 16.____
Of the following, it would be BEST if you responded by saying:

   A. *"Let me review my records to see if I have assigned the work fairly, and I will get right back to you."*
   B. *"I have given a lot of thought to how assignments are allocated, and it is fair for everyone. Please go back to work."*
   C. *"Last week you complained about needing a new electric stapler. The week before, you said you lost money in the vending machine. Isn't there anything you like around here?"*
   D. *"I am really sorry things have worked out this way, but I have to ask you to do the work anyway."*

17. Morgan works very, very hard but is not as productive as he could be, considering how hard he works. He seems to have a hard time setting priorities and determining what is really important. There have been a number of occasions when you have found him hard at work on projects that were of much lower priority than others that were sitting on his desk. He also loves to collect information and thinks tons of information (some relevant, some not) will help him make the *perfect decision.* 17.____
If you were Morgan's supervisor, which of the following do you feel would be the BEST way to handle the above situation?

   A. Sit down with him and assist him in improving his decision–making skills.
   B. Meet with him to discuss your observations and then review his projects, establish priorities, and set realistic goals together
   C. Have him attend a training course on improving self–esteem
   D. Have him attend a training program on improving decision–making skills

18. *A few years back, I had the occasion to work at an agency where a new manager came in. We soon found out that the happy atmosphere we had all enjoyed for the past few years was slowly eroding. We started receiving memos for everything and anything; such as no more placing sweaters on chairs, absolutely clear desk tops, personal chattering is forbidden at all times, compulsory signing in and out at lunch time, and so on. This soon brought a big change in our health. We got nervous stomachs, headaches, high blood pressure, and so on. He also stated that women were taking men's jobs away and should be at home. Many of us spoke to the higher-ups, but nothing was done. So now I had to make a big decision. I loved my job but not the atmosphere I was working in. I was fortunate in having a friend who helped me to get into another agency where I still work. This atmosphere caused quite a few more people to leave, and it was a big shame because we all were good, productive workers. In fact, in many cases the agency had to hire two workers to do the job one of us had been able to do so well.* 18.____
What could the administrators have done to avoid the above situation?

A. Conducted exit interviews of the employees who left to determine their reasons for leaving
B. Instituted the above changes more slowly
C. Realized the changes were hurting employee morale and withdrawn them
D. Used the carrot-and-stick approach to management

19. John is a 25-year-old black training specialist trainee in Agency X. He has been with the agency for eight months. John works with Ed, a 28-year-old white training specialist who has been in his position for four years. Their supervisor is Daniel, a 30-year-old white male who has been supervisor for six years. Daniel and Ed are good friends. John has become upset because he and Ed are treated so differently. Ed is allowed to come in late and leave early. On days when Ed drives his car to the office, he is allowed to leave every 90 minutes to change his parking place so that he won't get a parking ticket. Ed never has to let Daniel know where he is going or what meetings he is attending. John is not allowed any leave violations, however minor. The second time he was a few minutes late to work, Daniel called him in to his office and reprimanded him. There is a training conference in Washington, D.C. that Ed and Daniel are going to. John has asked permission to go, but has been told he cannot go because he would not benefit as much as Ed and Daniel would. 19.___
Of the following statements, which BEST applies to the above paragraph?

A. Bad supervision can look a lot like discrimination.
B. Friends should never work together.
C. Agencies should provide parking for their employees in order to improve productivity and reduce friction.
D. Supervisors should be careful in choosing when to reprimand employees.

20. All of the following are common problems faced by new supervisors EXCEPT: 20.___

A. One's former peers are now people one has to supervise, and this can lead to confusion, conflict, or resentment
B. The supervisor may have been *top dog* in the previous title and now has to start at the *bottom* in the new position; this can lead to arrogant or defensive behavior
C. New supervisors usually experience low levels of stress
D. The new supervisor is often selected because he or she was a very competent employee, not because he or she demonstrated leadership or supervisory skills, and the lack of these skills can lead to serious problems with those he or she supervises

KEY (CORRECT ANSWERS)

1.	A	11.	D
2.	A	12.	A
3.	D	13.	A
4.	A	14.	A
5.	C	15.	C
6.	B	16.	A
7.	B	17.	B
8.	A	18.	C
9.	B	19.	A
10.	B	20.	C

REPORT WRITING

EXAMINATION SECTION

TEST 1

DIRECTIONS: Each question or incomplete statement is followed by several suggested answers or completions. Select the one that BEST answers the question or completes the statement. *PRINT THE LETTER OF THE CORRECT ANSWER IN THE SPACE AT THE RIGHT.*

Questions 1-4.

DIRECTIONS: Answer Questions 1 through 4 on the basis of the following report which was prepared by a supervisor for inclusion in his agency's annual report.

Line #

On Oct. 13, I was assigned to study the salaries paid. to clerical employees in various titles by the city and by private industry in the area.

In order to get the data I needed, I called Mr. Johnson at the Bureau of the Budget and the payroll officers at X Corp.— a brokerage house, Y Co. —an insurance company, and Z Inc. — a publishing firm. None of them was available and I had to call all of them again the next day.

When I finally got the information I needed, I drew up a chart, which is attached. Note that not all of the companies I contacted employed people at all the different levels used in the city service.

The conclusions I draw from analyzing this information is as follows: The city's entry-level salary is about average for the region; middle-level salaries are generally higher in the city government plan than in private industry; but salaries at the highest levels in private industry are better than city employees' pay.

1. Which of the following criticisms about the style in which this report is written is MOST valid? 1.____
   A. It is too informal.
   B. It is too concise.
   C. It is too choppy.
   D. The syntax is too complex.

2. Judging from the statements made in the report, the method followed by this employee in performing his research was 2.____
   A. *good*; he contacted a representative sample of businesses in the area
   B. *poor*; he should have drawn more definite conclusions
   C. *good*; he was persistent in collecting information
   D. *poor*; he did not make a thorough study

3. One sentence in this report contains a grammatical error. This sentence begins on line number 3.____
   A. 4 B. 7 C. 10 D. 14

4. The type of information given in this report which should be presented in footnotes or in an appendix is the 4.____
   A. purpose of the study
   B. specifics about the businesses contacted
   C. reference to the chart
   D. conclusions drawn by the author

5. The use of a graph to show statistical data in a report is SUPERIOR to a table because it 5.____
   A. features approximations
   B. emphasizes facts and relationships more dramatically
   C. presents data more accurately
   D. is easily understood by the average reader

6. Of the following, the degree of formality required of a written report in tone is MOST likely to depend on the 6.____
   A. subject matter of the report
   B. frequency of its occurrence
   C. amount of time available for its preparation
   D. audience for whom the report is intended

7. Of the following, a distinguishing characteristic of a written report intended for the head of your agency as compared to a report prepared for a lower-echelon staff member is that the report for the agency head should USUALLY include 7.____
   A. considerably more detail, especially statistical data
   B. the essential details in an abbreviated form
   C. all available source material
   D. an annotated bibliography

8. Assume that you are asked to write a lengthy report for use by the administrator of your agency, the subject of which is "The Impact of Proposed New Data Processing Operation on Line Personnel" in your agency. You decide that the *most* appropriate type of report for you to prepare is an analytical report, including recommendations. 8.____
   The MAIN reason for your decision is that
   A. the subject of the report is extremely complex
   B. large sums of money are involved
   C. the report is being prepared for the administrator
   D. you intend to include charts and graphs

9. Assume that you are preparing a report based on a survey dealing with the attitudes of employees in Division X regarding proposed new changes in compensating employees for working overtime. Three percent of the respondents to the survey voluntarily offer an unfavorable opinion on the method of assigning overtime work, a question not specifically asked of the employees. 9.____
On the basis of this information, the MOST appropriate and significant of the following comments for you to make in the report with regard to employees' attitudes on assigning overtime work is that
   A. an insignificant percentage of employees dislike the method of assigning overtime work
   B. three percent of the employees in Division X dislike the method of assigning overtime work
   C. three percent of the sample selected for the survey voiced an unfavorable opinion on the method of assigning overtime work
   D. some employees voluntarily voiced negative feelings about the method of assigning overtime work, making it impossible to determine the extent of this attitude

10. A supervisor should be able to prepare a report that is well-written and unambiguous. 10.____
Of the following sentences that might appear in a report, select the one which communicates MOST clearly the intent of its author.
   A. When your subordinates speak to a group of people, they should be well-informed.
   B. When he asked him to leave, SanMan King told him that he would refuse the request.
   C. Because he is a good worker, Foreman Jefferson assigned Assistant Foreman D'Agostino to replace him.
   D. Each of us is responsible for the actions of our subordinates.

11. In some reports, especially longer ones, a list of the resources (books, papers, magazines, etc.) used to prepare it is included. This list is called the 11.____
   A. accreditation
   B. bibliography
   C. summary
   D. glossary

12. Reports are usually divided into several sections, some of which are more necessary than others. 12.____
Of the following, the section which is ABSOLUTELY necessary to include in a report is
   A. a table of contents
   B. the body
   C. an index
   D. a bibliography

13. Suppose you are writing a report on an interview you have just completed with a particularly hostile applicant. 13.____
Which of the following BEST describes what you should include in this report?
   A. What you think caused the applicant's hostile attitude during the interview
   B. Specific examples of the applicant's hostile remarks and behavior
   C. The relevant information uncovered during the interview
   D. A recommendation that the applicant's request be denied because of his hostility

14. When including recommendations in a report to your supervisor, which of the following is MOST important for you to do? 14.____
   A. Provide several alternative courses of action for each recommendation
   B. First present the supporting evidence, then the recommendations
   C. First present the recommendations, then the supporting evidence
   D. Make sure the recommendations arise logically out of the information in the report

15. It is often necessary that the writer of a report present facts and sufficient arguments to gain acceptance of the points, conclusions, or recommendations set forth in the report. 15.____
Of the following, the LEAST advisable step to take in organizing a report, when such argumentation is the important factor, is a(n)
   A. elaborate expression of personal belief
   B. businesslike discussion of the problem as a whole
   C. orderly arrangement of convincing data
   D. reasonable explanation of the primary issues

16. In some types of reports, visual aids add interest, meaning, and support. They also provide an essential means of effectively communicating the message of the report. 16.____
Of the following, the selection of the suitable visual aids to use with a report is LEAST dependent on the
   A. nature and scope of the report
   B. way in which the aid is to be used
   C. aid used in other reports
   D. prospective readers of the report

17. Visual aids used in a report may be placed either in the text material or in the appendix. 17.____
Deciding where to put a chart, table, or any such aid should depend on the
   A. title of the report
   B. purpose of the visual aid
   C. title of the visual aid
   D. length of the report

18. A report is often revised several times before final preparation and distribution in an effort to make certain the report meets the needs of the situation for which it is designed. 18.____
Which of the following is the BEST way for the author to be sure that a report covers the areas he intended?

TEST 2

DIRECTIONS: Each question or incomplete statement is followed by several suggested answers or completions. Select the one that BEST answers the question or completes the statement. *PRINT THE LETTER OF THE CORRECT ANSWER IN THE SPACE AT THE RIGHT.*

1. It is often necessary that the writer of a report present facts and sufficient arguments to gain acceptance of the points, conclusions, or recommendations set forth in the report. 1.____
   Of the following, the LEAST advisable step to take in organizing a report, when such argumentation is the important factor, is a(n)
   A. elaborate expression of personal belief
   B. businesslike discussion of the problem as a whole
   C. orderly arrangement of convincing data
   D. reasonable explanation of the primary issues

2. Of the following, the factor which is generally considered to be LEAST characteristic of a good control report is that it 2.____
   A. stresses performance that adheres to standard rather than emphasizing the exception
   B. supplies information intended to serve as the basis for corrective action
   C. provides feedback for the planning process
   D. includes data that reflect trends as well as current status

3. An administrative assistant has been asked by his superior to write a concise, factual report with objective conclusions and recommendations based on facts assembled by other researchers. 3.____
   Of the following factors, the administrative assistant should give LEAST consideration to
   A. the educational level of the person or persons for whom the report is being prepared
   B. the use to be made of the report
   C. the complexity of the problem
   D. his own feelings about the importance of the problem

4. When making a written report, it is often recommended that the findings or conclusions be presented near the beginning of the report. 4.____
   Of the following, the MOST important reason for doing this is that it
   A. facilitates organizing the material clearly
   B. assures that all the topics will be covered
   C. avoids unnecessary repetition of ideas
   D. prepares the reader for the facts that will follow

5. You have been asked to write a report on methods of hiring and training new employees. Your report is going to be about ten pages long. 5.____
For the convenience of your readers, a brief summary of your findings should
   A. appear at the beginning of your report
   B. be appended to the report as a postscript
   C. be circulated in a separate memo
   D. be inserted in tabular form in the middle of your report

6. In preparing a report, the MAIN reason for writing an outline is usually to 6.____
   A. help organize thoughts in a logical sequence
   B. provide a guide for the typing of the report
   C. allow the ultimate user to review the report in advance
   D. ensure that the report is being prepared on schedule

7. The one of the following which is MOST appropriate as a reason for including footnotes in a report is to 7.____
   A. correct capitalization
   B. delete passages
   C. improve punctuation
   D. cite references

8. A completed formal report may contain all of the following EXCEPT 8.____
   A. a synopsis
   B. a preface
   C. marginal notes
   D. bibliographical references

9. Of the following, the MAIN use of proofreaders' marks is to 9.____
   A. explain corrections to be made
   B. indicate that a manuscript has been read and approved
   C. let the reader know who proofread the report
   D. indicate the format of the report

10. Informative, readable, and concise reports have been found to observe the following rules: 10.____
   Rule I. Keep the report short and easy to understand
   Rule II. Vary the length of sentences.
   Rule III. Vary the style of sentences so that, for example, they are not all just subject-verb, subject-verb.

Consider this hospital laboratory report: The experiment was started in January. The apparatus was put together in six weeks. At that time, the synthesizing process was begun. The synthetic chemicals were separated. Then they were used in tests on patients.
Which one of the following choices MOST accurately classifies the above rules into those which are violated by this report ad those which are not?
   A. II is violated, but I and III are not.
   B. III is violated, but I and II are not.
   C. II and III are violated, but I is not.
   D. I, II, and III are violated,

Questions 11-13.

DIRECTIONS: Questions 11 through 13 are based on the following example of a report. The report consists of eight numbered sentences, some of which are not consistent with the principles of good report writing.

(1) I interviewed Mrs. Loretta Crawford in Room 424 of County Hospital. (2) She had collapsed on the street and been brought into emergency. (3) She is an attractive woman with many friends judging by the cards she had received. (4) She did not know what her husband's last job had been, or what their present income was. (5) The first thing that Mrs. Crawford said was that she had never worked and that her husband was presently unemployed. (6) She did not know if they had any medical coverage or if they could pay the bill. (7) She said that her husband could not be reached by telephone but that he would be in to see her that afternoon. (8) I left word at the nursing station to be called when he arrived.

11. A good report should be arranged in logical order. 11.____
Which of the following sentences from the report does NOT appear in its proper sequence in the report?
A. 1 B. 4 C. 7 D. 8

12. Only material that is relevant to the main thought of a report should be included. 12.____
Which of the following sentences from the report contains material which is LEAST relevant to this report? Sentence
A. 3 B. 4 C. 6 D. 8

13. Reports should include all essential information. 13.____
Of the following, the MOST important fact that is missing from this report is:
A. Who was involved in the interview
B. What was discovered at the interview
C. When the interview took place
D. Where the interview took place

Questions 14-15.

DIRECTIONS: Each of Questions 14 and 15 consists of four numbered sentences which constitute a paragraph in a report. They are not in the right order. Choose the numbered arrangement appearing after letter A, B, C, or D which is MOST logical and which BEST expresses the thought of the paragraph.

14. I. Congress made the commitment explicit in the Housing Act of 1949, establishing as a national goal the realization of a decent home and suitable environment for every American family. 14.____
II. The result has been that the goal of decent home and suitable environment is still as far distant as ever for the disadvantaged urban family
III. In spite of this action by Congress, federal housing programs have continued to be fragmented and grossly under-funded.
IV. The passage of the National Housing Act signaled a new federal commitment to provide housing for the nation's citizens.

The CORRECT answer is:
A. I, IV, III, II B. IV, I, III, II C. IV, I, III, II D. II, IV, I, III

15. I. The greater expense does not necessarily involve "exploitation," but it is often perceived as exploitative and unfair by those who are aware of the price differences involved, but unaware of operating costs. 15.____
II. Ghetto residents believe they are "exploited" by local merchants, and evidence substantiates some of these beliefs.
III. However, stores in low-income areas were more likely to be small independents, which could not achieve the economies available to supermarket chains and were, therefore, more likely to charge higher prices, and the customers were more likely to buy smaller-sized packages which are more expensive per unit of measure.
IV. A study conducted in one city showed that distinctly higher prices were charged for goods sold in ghetto stores than in other areas.

The CORRECT answer is:
A. IV, II, I, III B. IV, I, III, II C. II, IV, III, I D. II, III, IV, I

16. In organizing data to be presented in a formal report, the FIRST of the following steps should be 16.____
A. determining the conclusions to be drawn
B. establishing the time sequence of the data
C. sorting and arranging like data into groups
D. evaluating how consistently the data support the recommendations

17. All reports should be prepared with at least one copy so that 17.____
A. there is one copy for your file
B. there is a copy for your supervisor
C. the report can be sent to more than one person
D. the person getting the report can forward a copy to someone else

18. Before turning in a report of an investigation he has made, a supervisor discovers some additional information he did not include in this report. Whether he rewrites this report to include this additional information should PRIMARILY depend on the 18.____
A. importance of the report itself
B. number of people who will eventually review this report
C. established policy covering the subject matter of the report
D. bearing this new information has on the conclusions of the report

KEY (CORRECT ANSWERS)

1.	A	11.	B
2.	A	12.	A
3.	D	13.	C
4.	D	14.	B
5.	A	15.	C
6.	A	16.	C
7.	D	17.	A
8.	C	18.	D
9.	A		
10.	C		

EVALUATING CONCLUSIONS IN LIGHT OF KNOWN FACTS

EXAMINATION SECTION

TEST 1

DIRECTIONS: Each question or incomplete statement is followed by several suggested answers or completions. Select the one that BEST answers the question or completes the statement. *PRINT THE LETTER OF THE CORRECT ANSWER IN THE SPACE AT THE RIGHT.*

Questions 1-9.

DIRECTIONS: In Questions 1 through 9, you will read a set of facts and a conclusion drawn from them. The conclusion may be valid or invalid, based on the facts. It is your task to determine the validity of the conclusion.
For each question, select the letter before the statement that BEST expresses the relationship between the given facts and the conclusion that has been drawn from them. Your choices are:

A. The facts prove the conclusion.
B. The facts disprove the conclusion; or
C. The facts neither prove nor disprove the conclusion.

1. FACTS: Lauren must use Highway 29 to get to work. Lauren has a meeting today at 9:00 A.M. If she misses the meeting, Lauren will probably lose a major account. Highway 29 is closed all day today for repairs. 1.____

CONCLUSION: Lauren will not be able to get to work.

A. The facts prove the conclusion.
B. The facts disprove the conclusion.
C. The facts neither prove nor disprove the conclusion.

2. FACTS: The Tumbleweed Follies, a traveling burlesque show, is looking for a new line dancer. The position requires both singing and dancing skills. If the show cannot fill the position by Friday, it will begin to look for a magician to fill the time slot currently held by the line dancers. Willa, who wants to audition for the line dancing position, can sing, but cannot dance. 2.____

CONCLUSION: Willa is qualified to audition for the part of line dancer.

A. The facts prove the conclusion.
B. The facts disprove the conclusion.
C. The facts neither prove nor disprove the conclusion.

3. FACTS: Terry owns two dogs, Spike and Stan. One of the dogs is short-haired and has blue eyes. One dog as a pink nose. The blue-eyed dog never barks. One of the dogs has white fur on its paws. Sam has long hair. 3.____

CONCLUSION: Spike never barks.

A. The facts prove the conclusion.
B. The facts disprove the conclusion.
C. The facts neither prove nor disprove the conclusion.

4. FACTS: No science teachers are members of the PTA. Some English teachers are members of the PTA. Some English teachers in the PTA also wear glasses. Every PTA member is required to sit on the dunking stool at the student carnival except for those who wear glasses, who will be exempt. Those who are exempt, however, will have to officiate the hamster races. All of the English teachers in the PTA who do not wear glasses are married. 4.____

CONCLUSION: All the married English teachers in the PTA will set on the dunking stool at the student carnival.

A. The facts prove the conclusion.
B. The facts disprove the conclusion.
C. The facts neither prove nor disprove the conclusion.

5. FACTS: If the price of fuel is increased and sales remain constant, oil company profits will increase. The price of fuel was increased, and market experts project that sales levels are likely to be maintained. 5.____

CONCLUSION: The price of fuel will increase.

A. The facts prove the conclusion.
B. The facts disprove the conclusion.
C. The facts neither prove nor disprove the conclusion.

6. FACTS: Some members of the gymnastics team are double-jointed, and some members of the gymnastics team ae also on the lacrosse team. Some double-jointed members of the gymnastics team are also coaches. All gymnastics team members perform floor exercises, except the coaches. All the double-jointed members of the gymnastics team who are not coaches are freshmen. 6.____

CONCLUSION: Some double-jointed freshmen are coaches.

A. The facts prove the conclusion.
B. The facts disprove the conclusion.
C. The facts neither prove nor disprove the conclusion.

7. FACTS: Each member of the International Society speaks at least one foreign language, but no member speaks more than four foreign languages. Five members speak Spanish; three speak Mandarin; four speak French; four speak German; and five speak a foreign language other than Spanish, Mandarin, French, or German. 7.____

CONCLUSION: The lowest possible number of members in the International Society is eight.

A. The facts prove the conclusion.
B. The facts disprove the conclusion.
C. The facts neither prove nor disprove the conclusion.

8. FACTS: Mary keeps seven cats in her apartment. Only three of the cats will eat the same kind of food. Mary wants to keep at least one extra bag of each kind of food. 8.____

CONCLUSION: The minimum number of bags Mary will need to keep as extra is 7.

A. The facts prove the conclusion.
B. The facts disprove the conclusion.
C. The facts neither prove nor disprove the conclusion.

9. FACTS: In Ed and Marie's exercise group, everyone likes the treadmill or the stationary bicycle, or both, but Ed does not like the stationary bicycle. Marie has not expressed a preference, but spends most of her time on the stationary bicycle. 9.____

CONCLUSION: Everyone in the group who does not like the treadmill likes the stationary bicycle.

A. The facts prove the conclusion.
B. The facts disprove the conclusion.
C. The facts neither prove nor disprove the conclusion.

Questions 10-17.

DIRECTIONS: Questions 10 through 17 are based on the following reading passage. It is not your knowledge of the particular topic that is being tested, but your ability to reason based on what you have read. The passage is likely to detail several proposed courses of action and factors affecting these proposals. The reading passage is followed by a conclusion or outcome based on the facts in the passage, or a description of a decision taken regarding the situation. The conclusion is followed by a number of statements that have a possible connection to the conclusion. For each statement, you are to determine whether:

A. The statement proves the conclusion.
B. The statement supports the conclusion but does not prove it.
C. The statement disproves the conclusion.
D. The statement weakens the conclusion but does not disprove it.
E. The statement has no relevance to the conclusion.

Remember that the conclusion after the passage is to be accepted as the outcome of what actually happened, and that you are being asked to evaluate the impact each statement would have had on the conclusion.

PASSAGE

The Owyhee Mission School District's Board of Directors is hosting a public meeting to debate the merits of the proposed abolition of all bilingual education programs within the district. The group that has made the proposal believes the programs, which teach immigrant children academic subjects in their native language until they have learned English well enough to join mainstream classes, inhibit the ability of students to acquire English quickly and succeed in school and in the larger American society. Such programs, they argue, are also a wasteful drain on the district's already scant resources.

At the meeting, several teachers and parents stand to speak out against the proposal. The purpose of an education, they say, should be to build upon, rather than dismantle, a minority child's language and culture. By teaching children in academic subjects in their native tongues, while simultaneously offering English language instruction, schools can meet the goals of learning English and progressing through academic subjects along with their peers.

Hiram Nguyen, a representative of the parents whose children are currently enrolled in bilingual education, stands at the meeting to express the parents' wishes. The parents have been polled, he says, and are overwhelmingly of the opinion that while language and culture are important to them, they are not things that will disappear from the students' lives if they are no longer taught in the classroom. The most important issue for the parents is whether their children will succeed in school and be competitive in the larger American society. If bilingual education can be demonstrated to do that, then the parents are in favor of continuing it.

At the end of the meeting, a proponent of the plan, Oscar Ramos, stands to clarify some misconceptions about the proposal. It does not call for a "sink or swim" approach, he says, but allows for an interpreter to be present in mainstream classes to explain anything a student finds too complex or confusing.

The last word of the meeting is given to Delia Cruz, a bilingual teacher at one of the district's elementary schools. A student is bound to find anything complex or confusing, she says, if it is spoken in a language he has never heard before. It is more wasteful to place children in classrooms where they don't understand anything, she says, than it is to try to teach them something useful as they are learning the English language.

CONCLUSION: After the meeting, the Owyhee Mission School District's Board of Directors votes to terminate all the district's bilingual education programs at the end of the current academic year, but to maintain the current level of funding to each of the schools that have programs cut.

10. A poll conducted by the *Los Angeles Times* at approximately the same time as the Board's meeting indicated that 75% of the people were opposed to bilingual education; among Latinos, opposition was 84%. 10.____
   A. The statement proves the conclusion.
   B. The statement supports the conclusion but does not prove it.
   C. The statement disproves the conclusion.
   D. The statement weakens the conclusion but does not disprove it.
   E. The statement has no relevance to the conclusion.

11. Of all the studies connected on bilingual education programs, 64% indicate that students learned English grammar better in "sink or swim" classes without any special features than they did in bilingual education classes. 11.____
   A. The statement proves the conclusion.
   B. The statement supports the conclusion but does not prove it.
   C. The statement disproves the conclusion.
   D. The statement weakens the conclusion but does not disprove it.
   E. The statement has no relevance to the conclusion.

12. In the academic year that begins after the Board's vote, Montgomery Burns Elementary, an Owyhee Mission District school, launches a new bilingual program for the children of Somali immigrants. 12.____
   A. The statement proves the conclusion.
   B. The statement supports the conclusion but does not prove it.
   C. The statement disproves the conclusion.
   D. The statement weakens the conclusion but does not disprove it.
   E. The statement has no relevance to the conclusion.

13. In the previous academic year, under severe budget restraints, the Owyhee Mission District cut all physical education, music, and art classes, but its funding for bilingual education classes increased by 18%. 13.____
   A. The statement proves the conclusion.
   B. The statement supports the conclusion but does not prove it.
   C. The statement disproves the conclusion.
   D. The statement weakens the conclusion but does not disprove it.
   E. The statement has no relevance to the conclusion.

14. Before the Board votes, a polling consultant conducts randomly sampled assessments of immigrant students who enrolled in Owyhee District schools at a time when they did not speak any English at all. Ten years after graduating from high school, 44% of those who received bilingual education were professionals – doctors, lawyers, educators, engineers, etc. Of those who did not receive bilingual education, 38% were professionals. 14.____
   A. The statement proves the conclusion.
   B. The statement supports the conclusion but does not prove it.
   C. The statement disproves the conclusion.
   D. The statement weakens the conclusion but does not disprove it.
   E. The statement has no relevance to the conclusion.

15. Over the past several years, the scores of Owyhee District students have gradually declined, and enrollment numbers have followed as anxious parents transferred their children to other schools or applied for a state-funded voucher program. 15.____
   A. The statement proves the conclusion.
   B. The statement supports the conclusion but does not prove it.
   C. The statement disproves the conclusion.
   D. The statement weakens the conclusion but does not disprove it.
   E. The statement has no relevance to the conclusion.

16. California and Massachusetts, two of the most liberal states in the country, have each passed ballot measures banning bilingual education in public schools. 16.____
   A. The statement proves the conclusion.
   B. The statement supports the conclusion but does not prove it.
   C. The statement disproves the conclusion.
   D. The statement weakens the conclusion but does not disprove it.
   E. The statement has no relevance to the conclusion.

17. In the academic year that begins after the Board's vote, no Owyhee Mission Schools are conducting bilingual instruction. 17.____
   A. The statement proves the conclusion.
   B. The statement supports the conclusion but does not prove it.
   C. The statement disproves the conclusion.
   D. The statement weakens the conclusion but does not disprove it.
   E. The statement has no relevance to the conclusion.

Questions 18-25.

DIRECTIONS: Questions 18 through 25 each provide four factual statements and a conclusion based on these statements. After reading the entire question, you will decide whether:
   A. The conclusion is proved by Statements 1-4;
   B. The conclusion is disproved by Statements 1-4;
   C. The facts are not sufficient to prove or disprove the conclusion.

18. FACTUAL STATEMENTS: 18.____
   1) Gear X rotates in a clockwise direction if Switch C is in the OFF position.
   2) Gear X will rotate in a counter-clockwise direction if Switch C is ON.
   3) If Gear X is rotating in a clockwise direction, then Gear Y will not be rotating at all.
   4) Switch C is OFF.

   CONCLUSION: Gear Y is rotating.

   A. The conclusion is proved by Statements 1-4;
   B. The conclusion is disproved by Statements 1-4;
   C. The facts are not sufficient to prove or disprove the conclusion.

19. FACTUAL STATEMENTS: 19.____
    1) Mark is older than Jim but younger than Dan.
    2) Fern is older than Mark but younger than Silas.
    3) Dan is younger than Silas but older than Edward.
    4) Edward is older than Mark but younger than Fern.

    CONCLUSION: Dan is older than Fern.

    A. The conclusion is proved by Statements 1-4;
    B. The conclusion is disproved by Statements 1-4;
    C. The facts are not sufficient to prove or disprove the conclusion.

20. FACTUAL STATEMENTS: 20.____
    1) Each of Fred's three sofa cushions lies on top of four lost coins.
    2) The cushion on the right covers two pennies and two dimes.
    3) The middle cushion covers two dimes and two quarters.
    4) The cushion on the left covers two nickels and two quarters.

    CONCLUSION: To be guaranteed of retrieving at least one coin of each denomination, and without looking at any of the coins, Frank must take three coins each from under the cushions on the right and the left.

    A. The conclusion is proved by Statements 1-4;
    B. The conclusion is disproved by Statements 1-4;
    C. The facts are not sufficient to prove or disprove the conclusion.

21. FACTUAL STATEMENTS: 21.____
    1) The door to the hammer mill chamber is locked if light 6 is red.
    2) The door to the hammer mill chamber is locked only when the mill is operating.
    3) If the mill is not operating, light 6 is blue.
    4) The door to the hammer mill chamber is locked.

    CONCLUSION: The mill is in operation.

    A. The conclusion is proved by Statements 1-4;
    B. The conclusion is disproved by Statements 1-4;
    C. The facts are not sufficient to prove or disprove the conclusion.

22. FACTUAL STATEMENTS: 22.____
    1) In a five-story office building, where each story is occupied by a single professional, Dr. Kane's office is above Dr. Assad's.
    2) Dr. Johnson's office is between Dr. Kane's and Dr. Conlon's.
    3) Dr. Steen's office is between Dr. Conlon's and Dr. Assad's.
    4) Dr. Johnson is on the fourth story.

    CONCLUSION: Dr. Steen occupies the second story.

A. The conclusion is proved by Statements 1-4;
B. The conclusion is disproved by Statements 1-4;
C. The facts are not sufficient to prove or disprove the conclusion.

23. FACTUAL STATEMENTS: 23.____
1) On Saturday, farmers Hank, Earl, Roy, and Cletus plowed a total of 520 acres.
2) Hank plowed twice as many acres as Roy.
3) Roy plowed half as much as the farmer who plowed the most.
4) Cletus plowed 160 acres.

CONCLUSION: Hank plowed 200 acres.
A. The conclusion is proved by Statements 1-4;
B. The conclusion is disproved by Statements 1-4;
C. The facts are not sufficient to prove or disprove the conclusion.

24. FACTUAL STATEMENTS: 24.____
1) Four travelers – Tina, Jodie, Alex, and Oscar – each traveled to a different island – Aruba, Jamaica, Nevis, and Barbados – but not necessarily respectively.
2) Tina did not travel as far to Jamaica as Jodie traveled to her island.
3) Oscar traveled twice as far as Alex, who traveled the same distance as the traveler who went to Aruba.
4) Oscar went to Barbados.

CONCLUSION: Oscar traveled the farthest.

A. The conclusion is proved by Statements 1-4;
B. The conclusion is disproved by Statements 1-4;
C. The facts are not sufficient to prove or disprove the conclusion.

25. FACTUAL STATEMENT: 25.____
1) In the natural history museum, every Native American display that contains pottery also contains beadwork.
2) Some of the displays containing lodge replicas also contain beadwork.
3) The display on the Choctaw, a Native American tribe, contains pottery.
4) The display on the Modoc, a Native American tribe, contains only two of these items.

CONCLUSION: If the Modoc display contains pottery, it does not contain lodge replicas.

A. The conclusion is proved by Statements 1-4;
B. The conclusion is disproved by Statements 1-4;
C. The facts are not sufficient to prove or disprove the conclusion.

KEY (CORRECT ANSWERS)

1.	A	11.	B
2.	B	12.	C
3.	A	13.	B
4.	A	14.	D
5.	C	15.	E
6.	B	16.	E
7.	B	17.	A
8.	B	18.	B
9.	A	19.	C
10.	B	20.	A

21. A
22. A
23. C
24. A
25. A

TEST 2

DIRECTIONS: Each question or incomplete statement is followed by several suggested answers or completions. Select the one that BEST answers the question or completes the statement. *PRINT THE LETTER OF THE CORRECT ANSWER IN THE SPACE AT THE RIGHT.*

Questions 1-9.

DIRECTIONS: In Questions 1 through 9, you will read a set of facts and a conclusion drawn from them. The conclusion may be valid or invalid, based on the facts. It is your task to determine the validity of the conclusion.
For each question, select the letter before the statement that BEST expresses the relationship between the given facts and the conclusion that has been drawn from them. Your choices are:

A. The facts prove the conclusion.
B. The facts disprove the conclusion; or
C. The facts neither prove nor disprove the conclusion.

1. FACTS: If the maximum allowable income for Medicaid recipients is increased, the number of Medicaid recipients will increase. If the number of Medicaid recipients increases, more funds must be allocated to the Medicaid program, which will require a tax increase. Taxes cannot be approved without the approval of the legislature. The legislature probably will not approve a tax increase. 1.____

CONCLUSION: The maximum allowable income for Medicaid recipients will increase.

A. The facts prove the conclusion.
B. The facts disprove the conclusion; or
C. The facts neither prove nor disprove the conclusion.

2. FACTS: All the dentists on the baseball team are short. Everyone in the dugout is a dentist, but not everyone in the dugout is short. The baseball team is not made up of people of any particular profession. 2.____

CONCLUSION: Some people who are not dentists are in the dugout.

A. The facts prove the conclusion.
B. The facts disprove the conclusion; or
C. The facts neither prove nor disprove the conclusion.

3. FACTS: A taxi company's fleet is divided into two fleets. Fleet One contains cabs A, B, C, and D. Fleet Two contains E, F, G, and H. Each cab is either yellow or green. Five of the cabs are yellow. Cabs A and E are not both yellow. Either Cab C or F, or both, are not yellow. Cabs B and H are either both yellow or both green. 3.____

CONCLUSION: Cab H is green.

A. The facts prove the conclusion.
B. The facts disprove the conclusion; or
C. The facts neither prove nor disprove the conclusion.

4. FACTS: Most people in the skydiving club are not afraid of heights. Everyone in the skydiving club makes three parachute jumps a month. 4.____

CONCLUSION: At least one person who is afraid of heights makes three parachute jumps a month.

A. The facts prove the conclusion.
B. The facts disprove the conclusion; or
C. The facts neither prove nor disprove the conclusion.

5. FACTS: If the Board approves the new rule, the agency will move to a new location immediately. If the agency moves, five new supervisors will be immediately appointed. The Board has approved the new proposal. 5.____

CONCLUSION: No new supervisors were appointed.

A. The facts prove the conclusion.
B. The facts disprove the conclusion; or
C. The facts neither prove nor disprove the conclusion.

6. FACTS: All the workers at the supermarket chew gum when they sack groceries. Sometimes Lance, a supermarket worker, doesn't chew gum at all when he works. Another supermarket worker, Jenny, chews gum the whole time she is at work. 6.____

CONCLUSION: Jenny always sacks groceries when she is at work.

7. FACTS: Lake Lottawatta is bigger than Lake Tacomi. Lake Tacomi and Lake Ottawa are exactly the same size. All lakes in Montana are bigger than Lake Ottawa. 7.____

CONCLUSION: Lake Lottawatta is in Montana.

A. The facts prove the conclusion.
B. The facts disprove the conclusion; or
C. The facts neither prove nor disprove the conclusion.

8. FACTS: Two men, Cox and Taylor, are playing poker at a table. Taylor has a pair of aces in his hand. One man is smoking a cigar. One of them has no pairs in his hand and is wearing an eye patch. The man wearing the eye patch is smoking a cigar. One man is bald. 8.____

CONCLUSION: Cox is smoking a cigar.

A. The facts prove the conclusion.
B. The facts disprove the conclusion; or
C. The facts neither prove nor disprove the conclusion.

9. FACTS: All Kwakiutls are Wakashan Indians. All Wakashan Indians originated on Vancouver Island. The Nootka also originated on Vancouver Island. 9.____

CONCLUSION: Kwakiutls originated on Vancouver Island.

A. The facts prove the conclusion.
B. The facts disprove the conclusion; or
C. The facts neither prove nor disprove the conclusion.

Questions 10-17.

DIRECTIONS: Questions 10 through 17 are based on the following reading passage. It is not your knowledge of the particular topic that is being tested, but your ability to reason based on what you have read. The passage is likely to detail several proposed courses of action and factors affecting these proposals. The reading passage is followed by a conclusion or outcome based on the facts in the passage, or a description of a decision taken regarding the situation. The conclusion is followed by a number of statements that have a possible connection to the conclusion. For each statement, you are to determine whether:

A. The statement proves the conclusion.
B. The statement supports the conclusion but does not prove it.
C. The statement disproves the conclusion.
D. The statement weakens the conclusion but does not disprove it.
E. The statement has no relevance to the conclusion.

Remember that the conclusion after the passage is to be accepted as the outcome of what actually happened, and that you are being asked to evaluate the impact each statement would have had on the conclusion.

PASSAGE

The World Wide Web portal and search engine, HipBot, is considering becoming a subscription-only service, locking out nonsubscribers from the content on its web site. HipBot currently relies solely on advertising revenues.

HipBot's content director says that by taking in an annual fee from each customer, the company can both increase profits and provide premium content that no other portal can match.

The marketing director disagrees, saying that there is no guarantee that anyone who now visits the web site for free will agree to pay for the privilege of visiting it again. Most will probably simply use the other major portals. Also, HipBot's advertising clients will not be happy when they learn that the site will be viewed by a more limited number of people.

CONCLUSION: In January of 2016, the CEO of HipBot decides to keep the portal open to all web users, with some limited "premium content" available to subscribers who don't mind paying a little extra to access it. The company will aim to maintain, or perhaps increase, its advertising revenue.

10. In an independent marketing survey, 62% of respondents said they "strongly agree" with the following statement: "I almost never pay attention to advertisements that appear on the World Wide Web." 10.____
    A. The statement proves the conclusion.
    B. The statement supports the conclusion but does not prove it.
    C. The statement disproves the conclusion.
    D. The statement weakens the conclusion but does not disprove it.
    E. The statement has no relevance to the conclusion.

11. When it learns about the subscription-only debate going on at HipBot, Wernham Hogg Entertainment, one of HipBot's most reliable clients, says it will withdraw its ads and place them on a free web portal if HipBot decides to limit its content to subscribers. Wernham Hogg pays HipBot about $6 million annually – about 12% of HipBot's gross revenues – to run its ads online. 11.____
    A. The statement proves the conclusion.
    B. The statement supports the conclusion but does not prove it.
    C. The statement disproves the conclusion.
    D. The statement weakens the conclusion but does not disprove it.
    E. The statement has no relevance to the conclusion.

12. At the end of the second quarter of FY 2016, after continued stagnant profits, the CEO of HipBot assembles a blue ribbon commission to gather and analyze data on the costs, benefits, and feasibility of adding a limited amount of "premium" content to the HipBot portal. 12.____
    A. The statement proves the conclusion.
    B. The statement supports the conclusion but does not prove it.
    C. The statement disproves the conclusion.
    D. The statement weakens the conclusion but does not disprove it.
    E. The statement has no relevance to the conclusion.

13. In the following fiscal year, Wernham Hogg Entertainment, satisfied with the "hit counts" on HipBot's free web site, spends another $1 million on advertisements that will appear on web pages that are available to HipBot's "premium subscribers. 13.____
    A. The statement proves the conclusion.
    B. The statement supports the conclusion but does not prove it.
    C. The statement disproves the conclusion.
    D. The statement weakens the conclusion but does not disprove it.
    E. The statement has no relevance to the conclusion.

14. HipBot's information technology director reports that the engineers in his department have come up with a feature that will search not only individual web pages, but tie into other web-based search engines, as well, and then comb through all these results to find those most relevant to the user's search. 14.____

A. The statement proves the conclusion.
B. The statement supports the conclusion but does not prove it.
C. The statement disproves the conclusion.
D. The statement weakens the conclusion but does not disprove it.
E. The statement has no relevance to the conclusion.

15. In an independent marketing survey, 79% of respondents said they "strongly agree" with the following statement: "Many web sites are so dominated by advertisements these days that it is increasingly frustrating to find the content I want to read or see." 15.____
A. The statement proves the conclusion.
B. The statement supports the conclusion but does not prove it.
C. The statement disproves the conclusion.
D. The statement weakens the conclusion but does not disprove it.
E. The statement has no relevance to the conclusion.

16. After three years of studies at the federal level, the Department of Commerce releases a report suggesting that, in general, the only private "subscriber-only" web sites that do well financially are those with a very specialized user population. 16.____
A. The statement proves the conclusion.
B. The statement supports the conclusion but does not prove it.
C. The statement disproves the conclusion.
D. The statement weakens the conclusion but does not disprove it.
E. The statement has no relevance to the conclusion.

17. HipBot's own marketing research indicates that the introduction of premium content has the potential to attract new users to the HipBot portal. 17.____
A. The statement proves the conclusion.
B. The statement supports the conclusion but does not prove it.
C. The statement disproves the conclusion.
D. The statement weakens the conclusion but does not disprove it.
E. The statement has no relevance to the conclusion.

Questions 18-25.

DIRECTIONS: Questions 18 through 25 each provide four factual statements and a conclusion based on these statements. After reading the entire question, you will decide whether:
A. The conclusion is proved by Statements 1-4;
B. The conclusion is disproved by Statements 1-4;
C. The facts are not sufficient to prove or disprove the conclusion.

18. FACTUAL STATEMENTS: 18.____
    1) If the alarm goes off, Sam will wake up.
    2) If Tandy wakes up before 4:00, Linda will leave the bedroom and sleep on the couch.
    3) If Linda leaves the bedroom, she'll check the alarm to make sure it is working.
    4) The alarm goes off.

    CONCLUSION: Tandy woke up before 4:00.

    A. The conclusion is proved by Statements 1-4;
    B. The conclusion is disproved by Statements 1-4;
    C. The facts are not sufficient to prove or disprove the conclusion.

19. FACTUAL STATEMENTS: 19.____
    1) Four brothers are named Earl, John, Gary, and Pete.
    2) Earl and Pete are unmarried.
    3) John is shorter than the youngest of the four.
    4) The oldest brother is married, and is also the tallest.

    CONCLUSION: Pete is the youngest brother.

    A. The conclusion is proved by Statements 1-4;
    B. The conclusion is disproved by Statements 1-4;
    C. The facts are not sufficient to prove or disprove the conclusion.

20. FACTUAL STATEMENTS: 20.____
    1) Automobile engines are cooled either by air or by liquid.
    2) If the engine is small and simple enough, air from a belt-driven fan will cool it sufficiently.
    3) Most newer automobile engines are too complicated to be air-cooled.
    4) Air-cooled engines are cheaper and easier to build then liquid-cooled engines.

    CONCLUSION: Most newer automobile engines use liquid coolant.

    A. The conclusion is proved by Statements 1-4;
    B. The conclusion is disproved by Statements 1-4;
    C. The facts are not sufficient to prove or disprove the conclusion.

21. FACTUAL STATEMENTS: 21.____
    1) Erica will only file a lawsuit if she is injured while parasailing.
    2) If Rick orders Trip to run a rope test, Trip will check the rigging.
    3) If the rigging does not malfunction, Erica will not be injured.
    4) Rick orders Trip to run a rope test.

CONCLUSION: Erica does not file a lawsuit.

A. The conclusion is proved by Statements 1-4;
B. The conclusion is disproved by Statements 1-4;
C. The facts are not sufficient to prove or disprove the conclusion.

22. FACTUAL STATEMENTS: 22.____
1) On Maple Street, which is four blocks long, Bill's shop is two blocks east of Ken's shop.
2) Ken's shop is one block west of the only shop on Maple Street with an awning.
3) Erma's shop is one block west of the easternmost block.
4) Bill's shop is on the easternmost block.

CONCLUSION: Bill's shop has an awning.

A. The conclusion is proved by Statements 1-4;
B. The conclusion is disproved by Statements 1-4;
C. The facts are not sufficient to prove or disprove the conclusion.

23. FACTUAL STATEMENTS: 23.____
1) Gear X rotates in a clockwise direction if Switch C is in the OFF position.
2) Gear X will rotate in a counter-clockwise direction if Switch C is ON.
3) If Gear X is rotating in a clockwise direction, then Gear Y will not be rotating at all.
4) Gear Y is rotating.

CONCLUSION: Gear X is rotating in a counter-clockwise direction.

A. The conclusion is proved by Statements 1-4;
B. The conclusion is disproved by Statements 1-4;
C. The facts are not sufficient to prove or disprove the conclusion.

24. FACTUAL STATEMENTS: 24.____
1) The Republic of Garbanzo's currency system has four basic denominations: the pastor, the noble, the donner, and the rojo.
2) A pastor is worth 2 nobles.
3) 2 donners can be exchanged for a rojo.
4) 3 pastors are equal in value to 2 donners.

CONCLUSION: The rojo is most valuable.

A. The conclusion is proved by Statements 1-4;
B. The conclusion is disproved by Statements 1-4;
C. The facts are not sufficient to prove or disprove the conclusion.

25. FACTUAL STATEMENTS: 25.____
    1) At Prickett's Nursery, the only citrus trees left are either Meyer lemons or Valencia oranges, and every citrus tree left is either a dwarf or a semidwarf.
    2) Half of the semidwarf trees are Meyer lemons.
    3) There are more semidwarf trees left than dwarf trees.
    4) A quarter of the dwarf trees are Valencia oranges.

    CONCLUSION: There are more Valencia oranges left at Prickett's Nursery than Meyer lemons.

    A. The conclusion is proved by Statements 1-4;
    B. The conclusion is disproved by Statements 1-4;
    C. The facts are not sufficient to prove or disprove the conclusion.

KEY (CORRECT ANSWERS)

1.	C	11.	B
2.	B	12.	C
3.	B	13.	A
4.	A	14.	E
5.	B	15.	D
6.	C	16.	B
7.	C	17.	B
8.	A	18.	C
9.	A	19.	C
10.	E	20.	A

21.	C
22.	B
23.	C
24.	A
25.	B

LOGICAL REASONING
EVALUATING CONCLUSIONS IN LIGHT OF KNOWN FACTS

EXAMINATION SECTION

TEST 1

COMMENTARY

This section is designed to provide practice questions in evaluating conclusions when you are given specific data to work with.

We suggest you do the questions three at a time, consulting the answer key and then the solution section for any questions you may have missed. It's a good idea to try the questions again a week before the exam.

In the validity of conclusion type of question, you are first given a reading passage which describes a particular situation. The passage may be on any topic, as it is not your knowledge of the topic that is being tested, but your reasoning abilities. The passage is likely to detail several proposed courses of action and factors affecting these proposals. The reading passage is followed by a conclusion based on the facts in the passage, or a description of a decision taken regarding the situation. The conclusion is followed by a number of statements which have a possible connection to the conclusion. For each statement, you are to determine whether:

A. The statement proves the conclusion.
B. The statement supports the conclusion but does not prove it.
C. The statement disproves the conclusion.
D. The statement weakens the conclusion but does not disprove it.
E. The statement has no relevance to the conclusion.

Remember that the conclusion after the passage is to be accepted as the outcome of what actually happened, and that you are being asked to evaluate the impact each statement would have had on the conclusion.

Questions 1-8.

DIRECTIONS: Questions 1 through 8 are based on the following paragraph.

In May of 2018, Mr. Bryan inherited a clothing store on Main Street in a small New England town. The store has specialized in selling quality men's and women's clothing since 1920. Business has been stable throughout the years, neither increasing nor decreasing. He has an opportunity to buy two adjacent stores which would enable him to add a wider range and style of clothing. In order to do this, he would have to borrow a substantial amount of money. He also risks losing the goodwill of his present clientele.

CONCLUSION: On November 7, 2018, Mr. Bryan tells the owner of the two adjacent stores that he has decided not to purchase them. He feels that it would be best to simply maintain his present marketing position, as there would not be enough new business to support an expansion.

A. The statement proves the conclusion.
B. The statement supports the conclusion but does not prove it.
C. The statement disproves the conclusion.
D. The statement weakens the conclusion.
E. The statement is irrelevant to the conclusion.

1. A large new branch of the county's community college holds its first classes in September. 1.____

2. The town's largest factory shuts down with no indication that it will reopen. 2.____

3. The United States Census showed that the number of children per household dropped from 2.4 to 2.1 since the last census. 3.____

4. Mr. Bryan's brother tells him of a new clothing boutique specializing in casual women's clothing which is opening soon. 4.____

5. Mr. Bryan's sister buys her baby several items for Christmas at Mr. Bryan's store. 5.____

6. Mrs. McIntyre, the President of the Town Council, brings Mr. Bryan a home-baked pumpkin pie in honor of his store's 100th anniversary. They discuss the changes that have taken place in the town, and she comments on how his store has maintained the same look and feel over the years. 6.____

7. In October, Mr. Bryan's aunt lends him $50,000. 7.____

8. The Town Council has just announced that the town is eligible for funding from a federal project designed to encourage the location of new businesses in the central districts of cities and towns. 8.____

Questions 9-18.

DIRECTIONS: Questions 9 through 18 are based on the following paragraph.

A proposal was put before the legislative body of a country to require air bags in all automobiles manufactured for domestic use in that country after 2019. The air bag, made of nylon or plastic, is designed to inflate automatically within a car at the impact of a collision, thus protecting front-seat occupants from being thrown forward. There has been much support of the measure from consumer groups, the insurance industry, key legislators, and the general public. The country's automobile manufacturers, who contend the new crash equipment would add up to $1,000 to car prices and provide no more protection than existing seat belts, are against the proposed legislation

CONCLUSION: On April 21, 2014, the legislation requiring air bags in all automobiles manufactured for domestic use in that country after 2019.

A. The statement proves the conclusion.
B. The statement supports the conclusion but does not prove it.
C. The statement disproves the conclusion.
D. The statement weakens the conclusion.
E. The statement is irrelevant to the conclusion.

9. A study has shown that 59% of car occupants do not use seat belts. 9.____

10. The country's Department of Transportation has estimated that the crash protection equipment would save up to 5,900 lives each year. 10.____

11. On April 27, 2013, Augusta Raneoni was named head of an advisory committee to gather and analyze data on the costs, benefits, and feasibility of the proposed legislation on air bags in automobiles. 11.____

12. Consumer groups and the insurance industry accuse the legislature of rejecting passage of the regulation for political reasons. 12.____

13. A study by the Committee on Imports and Exports projected that the sales of imported cars would rise dramatically in 2019 because imported cars do not have to include air bags, and can be sold more cheaply. 13.____

14. Research has shown that air bags, if produced on a large scale, would cost about $200 apiece, and would provide more reliable protection than any other type of seat belt. 14.____

15. Auto sales in 2011 increased 3% over the previous year. 15.____

16. A Department of Transportation report in July of 2020 credits a drop in automobile deaths of 4,100 to the use of air bags. 16.____

17. In June of 2014, the lobbyist of the largest insurance company receives a bonus for her work on the passage of the air bag legislation. 17.____

18. In 2020, the stock in crash protection equipment has risen three-fold over the previous year. 18.____

Questions 19-25.

DIRECTIONS: Questions 19 through 25 are based on the following paragraph.

On a national television talk show, Joan Rivera, a famous comedienne, has recently insulted the physical appearances of a famous actress and the dead wife of an ex-President. There has been a flurry of controversy over her comments, and much discussion of the incident has appeared in the press. Most of the comments have been negative. It appears that this tie she might have gone too far. There have been cancellations of two of her five scheduled performances in the two weeks since the show was televised, and Joan's been receiving a lot of negative mail. Because of the controversy, she has an interview with a national news magazine at the end of the week, and her press agent is strongly urging her to apologize publicly. She feels strongly that her comments were no worse than any other she has ever made, and that the whole incident will *blow over* soon. She respects her press agent's judgment, however, as his assessment of public sentiment tends to be very accurate.

CONCLUSION: Joan does not apologize publicly, and during the interview she challenges the actress to a weight-losing contest. For every pound the actress loses, Joan says she will donate $1 to the Cellulite Prevention League.

A. The statement proves the conclusion.
B. The statement supports the conclusion but does not prove it.
C. The statement disproves the conclusion.
D. The statement weakens the conclusion.
E. The statement is irrelevant to the conclusion.

19. Joan's mother, who she is very fond of, is very upset with Joan's comments. 19.____

20. Six months after the interview, Joan's income has doubled. 20.____

21. Joan's agent is pleased with the way Joan handles the interview. 21.____

22. Joan's sister has been appointed Treasurer of the Cellulite Prevention League In her report, she states that Joan's $12 contribution is the only amount that has been donated to the League in its first six months. 22.____

23. The magazine receives many letters commending Joan for the courage it took for her to apologize publicly in the interview. 23.____

24. Immediately after the interview appears, another one of Joan's performances is cancelled. 24.____

25. Due to a printers' strike, the article was not published until the following week. 25.____

Questions 26-30.

DIRECTIONS: Questions 25 through 30 are based on the following paragraph.

The law-making body of Country X must decide what to do about the issue of recording television shows for home use. There is currently no law against recording shows directly from the TV as long as the DVDs are not used for commercial purposes. The increasing popularity of pay TV and satellite systems, combined with the increasing number of homes that own recording equipment, has caused a great deal of concern in some segments of the entertainment industry. Companies that own the rights to films, popular television shows, and sporting events feel that their copyright privileges are being violated, and they are seeking compensation or the banning of TV recording. Legislation has been introduced to make it illegal to record television programs for home use. Separate proposed legislation is also pending that would continue to allow recording of TV shows for home use, but would place a tax of 10% on each DVD that is purchased for home use. The income from that tax would then be proportionately distributed as royalties to those owning the rights to programs being aired. A weighted point system coupled with the averaging of several national viewing rating systems would be used to determine the royalties. There is a great deal of lobbying being done for both bills, as the manufacturers of DVDs and recording equipment are against the passage of the bills.

CONCLUSION: The legislature of Country X rejects both bills by a wide margin.

A. The statement proves the conclusion.
B. The statement supports the conclusion but does not prove it.
C. The statement disproves the conclusion.
D. The statement weakens the conclusion.
E. The statement is irrelevant to the conclusion.

26. Country X's Department of Taxation hires 500 new employees to handle the increased paperwork created by the new tax on DVDs. 26.____

27. A study conducted by the country's most prestigious accounting firm shows that the cost of implementing the proposed new DVD tax would be greater than the income expected from it. 27.____

28. It is estimated that 80% of all those working in the entertainment industry, excluding performers, own DVD recorders. 28.____

29. The head of Country X's law enforcement agency states that legislation banning the home recording of TV shows would be unenforceable. 29.____

30. Financial experts predict that unless a tax is placed on DVDs, several large companies in the entertainment industry will have to file for bankruptcy. 30.____

Questions 31-38.

DIRECTIONS: Questions 31 through 38 are variations on the type of question you just had. It is important that you read the question very carefully to determine exactly what is required.

31. In this question, select the choice that is MOST relevant to the conclusion. 31.____

I. The Buffalo Bills football team is in second place in its division.
II. The New England Patriots are in first place in the same division.
III. There are two games left to play in the season, and the Bills will not play the Patriots again.
IV. The New England Patriots won ten games and lost four games, and the Buffalo Bills have won eight games and lost six games.

CONCLUSION: The Buffalo Bills win their division.

A. The conclusion is proved by sentences I-IV.
B. The conclusion is disproved by sentences I-IV.
C. The facts are not sufficient to prove or disprove the conclusion.

32. In this question, select the choice that is MOST relevant to the conclusion. 32.____
I. On the planet of Zeinon there are only two different eye colors and only two different hair colors.
II. Half of those beings with purple hair have golden eyes.
III. There are more inhabitants with purple hair than there are inhabitants with silver hair.
IV. One-third of those with silver hair have green eyes.
CONCLUSION: There are more golden-eyed beings on Zeinon than green-eyed ones.
A. The conclusion is proved by sentences I-IV.
B. The conclusion is disproved by sentences I-IV.
C. The facts are not sufficient to prove or disprove the conclusion.

33. In this question, select the choice that is MOST relevant to the conclusion. 33.____
John and Kevin are leaving Amaranth to go to school in Bethany. They've decided to rent a small truck to move their possessions. Joe's Truck Rental charges $100 plus 30¢ a mile. National Movers charges $50 more but gives free mileage for the first 100 miles. After the first 100 miles, they charge 25¢ a mile.
CONCLUSION: John and Kevin rent their truck from National Movers because it is cheaper.
A. The conclusion is proved by the facts in the above paragraph.
B. The conclusion is disproved by the facts in the above paragraph.
C. The facts are not sufficient to prove or disprove the conclusion.

34. For this question, select the choice that supports the information given in the passage. 34.____
Municipalities in Country X are divided into villages, towns, and cities. A village has a population of 5,000 or less. The population of a town ranges from 5,001 to 15,000. In order to be incorporated as a city, the municipality must have a population over 15,000. If, after a village becomes a town, or a town becomes a city, the population drops below the minimum required (for example, the population of a city goes below 15,000), and stays below the minimum for more than ten years, it loses its current status, and drops to the next category. As soon as a municipality rises in population to the next category (village to town, for example), however, it is immediately reclassified to the next category.
In the 2000 census, Plainfield had a population of 12,000. Between 2000 and 2010, Plainfield grew 10%, and between 2010 and 2020 Plainfield grew another 20%. The population of Springdale doubled from 2000 to 2010, and increased 25% from 2010 to 2020. The city of Smallville's population, 20,283, has not changed significantly in recent years. Granton had a population of 25,000 people in1990, and has decreased 25% in each ten year period since then. Ellenville had a population of 4,283 in 1990, and grew 5% in each ten year period since 1990.

In 2020,

A. Plainfield, Smallville, and Granton are cities.
B. Smallville is a city, Granton is a town, and Ellenville is a village.
C. Springdale, Granton, and Ellenville are towns.
D. Plainfield and Smallville are cities, and Ellenville is a town.

35. For this question, select the choice that is MOST relevant to the conclusion. 35.____

A study was done for a major food-distributing firm to determine if there is any difference in the kind of caffeine containing products used by people of different ages. A sample of one thousand people between the ages of twenty and fifty were drawn from selected areas in the country. They were divided equally into three groups.

Those individuals who were 20-29 were designated Group A, those 30-39 were Group B, and those 40-50 were placed in Group C.

It was found that on the average, Group A drank 1.8 cups of coffee, Group B 3.1, and Group C 2.5 cups of coffee daily. Group A drank 2.1 cups of tea, Group B drank 1.2, and Group C drank 2.6 cups of tea daily. Group A drank 3 1.8 ounces glasses of cola, Group B drank 1.9, and Group C drank 1.5 glasses of cola daily.

CONCLUSION: According to the study, the average person in the 20-29 age group drinks less tea daily than the average person in the 40-50 age group, but drinks more coffee daily than the average person in the 30-39 age group drinks cola.

A. The conclusion is proved by the facts in the above paragraph.
B. The conclusion is disproved by the facts in the above paragraph.
C. The facts are not sufficient to prove or disprove the conclusion.

36. For this question, select the choice that is MOST relevant to the conclusion 36.____

I. Mary is taller than Jane but shorter than Dale.
II. Fred is taller than Mary but shorter than Steven.
III. Dale is shorter than Steven but taller than Elizabeth.
IV. Elizabeth is taller than Mary but not as tall as Fred.

CONCLUSION: Dale is taller than Fred.

A. The conclusion is proved by sentences I-IV.
B. The conclusion is disproved by sentences I-IV.
C. The facts are not sufficient to prove or disprove the conclusion.

37. For this question, select the choice that is MOST relevant to the conclusion. 37.____

I. Main Street is between Spring Street and Glenn Blvd.
II. Hawley Avenue is one block south of Spring Street and three blocks north of Main Street.
III. Glenn Street is five blocks south of Elm and four blocks south of Main.
IV. All the streets mentioned are parallel to one another.

CONCLUSION: Elm Street is between Hawley Avenue and Glenn Blvd.

A. The conclusion is proved by the facts in sentences I-IV.
B. The conclusion is disproved by the facts in sentences I-IV.
C. The facts are not sufficient to prove or disprove the conclusion.

38. For this question, select the choice that is MOST relevant to the conclusion. 38.____
   I. Train A leaves the town of Hampshire every day at 5:50 A.M. and arrives in New London at 6:42 A.M.
   II. Train A leaves New London at 7:00 A.M. and arrives in Kellogsville at 8:42 A.M.
   III. Train B leaves Kellogsville at 8:00 A.M. and arrives in Hampshire at 10:45 A.M.
   IV. Due to the need for repairs, there is just one railroad track between New London and Hampshire.

   CONCLUSION: It is impossible for Train A and Train B to follow these schedules without colliding.

   A. The conclusion is proved by the facts in sentences I-IV.
   B. The conclusion is disproved by the facts in sentences I-IV.
   C. The facts are not sufficient to prove or disprove the conclusion.

KEY (CORRECT ANSWERS)

1.	D	11.	C	21.	D	31.	C
2.	B	12.	C	22.	A	32.	A
3.	E	13.	D	23.	C	33.	C
4.	B	14.	B	24.	B	34.	B
5.	C	15.	E	25.	E	35.	B
6.	A	16.	B	26.	C	36.	C
7.	D	17.	A	27.	B	37.	A
8.	B	18.	B	28.	E	38.	B
9.	B	19.	D	29.	B		
10.	B	20.	E	30.	D		

SOLUTIONS TO QUESTIONS

1. The answer is D. This statement weakens the conclusion, but does not disprove it. If a new branch of the community college opened in September, it could possibly bring in new business for Mr. Bryant. Since it states in the conclusion that Mr. Bryant felt there would not be enough new business to support the additional stores, this would tend to disprove the conclusion. Choice C would not be correct because it's possible that he felt that the students would not have enough additional money to support his new venture, or would not be interested in his clothing styles. It's also possible that the majority of the students already live in the area, so that they wouldn't really be a new customer population. This type of question is tricky, and can initially be very confusing, so don't feel badly if you missed it. Most people need to practice with a few of these types of questions before they feel comfortable recognizing exactly what they're being asked to do.

2. The answer is B. It supports the conclusion because the closing of the factory would probably take money and customers out of the town, causing Mr. Bryant to lose some of his present business. It doesn't prove the conclusion, however, because we don't know how large the factory was. It's possible that only a small percentage of the population was employed there, or that they found other jobs.

3. The answer is E. The fact that the number of children per household dropped slightly nationwide in the decade is irrelevant. Statistics showing a drop nationwide doesn't mean that there was a drop in the number of children per household in Mr. Bryant's hometown. This is a tricky question, as choice B, supporting the conclusion but not proving it, may seem reasonable. If the number of children per household declined nationwide, then it may not seem unreasonable to feel that this would support Mr. Bryant's decision not to expand his business. However, we're preparing you for promotional exams, not "real life." One of the difficult things about taking exams is that sometimes you're forced to make a choice between two statements that both seem like they could be the possible answer. What you need to do in that case is choose the best choice. Becoming annoyed or frustrated with the question won't really help much. If there's a review of the exam, you can certainly appeal the question. There have been many cases where, after an appeal, two possible choices have been allowed as correct answers. We've included this question, however, to help you see what to do should you get a question like this. It's most important not to get rattled, and to select the BEST choice. In this case, the connection between the statistical information and Mr. Bryant's decision is pretty remote. If the question had said that the number of children in Mr. Bryant's <u>town</u> had decreased, then choice B would have been a more reasonable choice. It could also help in this situation to visualize the situation. Picture Mr. Bryant in his armchair reading that, nationwide, the average number of children per household has declined slightly. How likely would this be to influence his decision, especially since he sells men's and women's clothing? It would take a while for this decline in population to show up, and we're not even sure if it applies to Mr. Bryant's hometown. Don't feel badly if you missed this; it was tricky. The more of these you do, the more comfortable you'll feel.

4. The answer is B. If a new clothing boutique specializing in casual women's clothing were to open soon, this would lend support to Mr. Bryant's decision not to expand, but would not prove that he had actually made the decision to expand. A new women's clothing boutique would most likely be in competition with his existing business, thus making any possible expansion a riskier venture. We can't be sure from this, however, that he didn't go ahead and expand his business despite the increased competition. Choice A, proves the conclusion, would only be the answer if we could be absolutely sure from the statement that Mr. Bryant had actually not expanded his business.

5. The answer is C. This statement disproves the conclusion. In order for his sister to buy several items for her baby at Mr. Bryant's store, he would have to have changed his business to include children's clothing.

6. The answer is A. It definitely proves the conclusion. The passage states that Mr. Bryan's store had been in business since 1920. A pie baked in honor of his store's 100th anniversary would have to be presented sometime in 2020. The conclusion states that he made his decision not to expand on November 7, 2018. If, more than a year later Mrs. MacIntyre comments that his store has maintained the same look and feel over the years, it could not have been expanded, or otherwise significantly changed.

7. The answer is D. If Mr. Bryant's aunt lent him $50,000 in October, this would tend to weaken the conclusion, which took place in November. Because it was stated that Mr. Bryant would need to borrow money in order to expand his business, it would be logical to assume that if he borrowed money he had decided to expand his business, weakening the conclusion. The reason C, disproves the conclusion, is not the correct answer is because we can't be sure Mr. Bryant didn't borrow the money for another reason.

8. The answer is B. If Mr. Bryant's town is eligible for federal funds to encourage the location of new businesses in the central district, this would tend to support his decision not to expand his business. Funds to encourage new business would increase the likelihood of there being additional competition for Mr. Bryant's store to contend with. Since we can't say for sure that there would be direct competition from a new business, however, choice A would be incorrect. Note that this is also a tricky question. You might have thought that the new funds weakened the conclusion because it would mean that Mr. Bryant could easily get the money he needed. Mr. Bryant is expanding his present business, not creating a new business. Therefore, he is not eligible for the funding.

9. The answer is B. This is a very tricky question. It's stated that 59% of car occupants don't use seat belts. The legislature is considering the use of air bags because of safety issues. The advantage of air bags over seat belts is that they inflate upon impact, and don't require car occupants to do anything with them ahead of time. Since the population has strongly resisted using seat belts, the air bags could become even more important in saving lives. Since saving lives is the purpose of the proposed legislation, the information that a small percentage of people use seat belts could be helpful to the passage of the legislation. We can't be sure that this is reason enough for the legislature to vote for the legislation, however, so choice A in incorrect.

10. The answer is B, as the information that 5,900 lives could be saved would tend to support the conclusion. Saving that many lives through the use of air bags could be a very persuasive reason to vote for the legislation. Since we don't know for sure that it's enough of a compelling reason for the legislature to vote for the legislation, however, choice A could not be the answer.

11. The answer is C, disproves the conclusion. If the legislation had been passed as stated in the conclusion, there would be no reason to appoint someone head of an advisory committee six days later to analyze the "feasibility of the proposed legislation." The key word here is "proposed." If it has been proposed, it means it hasn't been passed. This contradicts the conclusion and, therefore, disproves it.

12. The answer is C, disproves the conclusion. If the legislation had passed, there would be no reason for supporters of the legislation to accuse the legislature of rejecting the legislation for political reasons. This question may have seemed so obvious that you might have thought there was a trick to it. Exams usually have a few obvious questions, which will trip you up if you begin reading too much into them.

13. The answer is D, as this would tend to disprove the conclusion. A projected dramatic rise in imported cars could be very harmful to the country's economy and could be a very good reason for some legislators to vote against the proposed legislation. It would be assuming too much to choose C, however, because we don't know if they actually did vote against it.

14. The answer is B. This information would tend to support the passage of the legislation. The estimate of the cost of the air bags is $800 less than the cost estimated by opponents, and it's stated that the protection would be more reliable than any other type of seat belt. Both of these would be good arguments in favor of passing the legislation. Since we don't know for sure, however, how persuasive they actually were, choice A would not be the correct choice.

15. The answer is E, as this is irrelevant information. It really doesn't matter whether auto sales in 2001 have increased slightly over the previous year. If the air bag legislation were to go into effect in 2004, that might make the information somehow more relevant. But the air bag legislation would not take effect until 2009, so the information is irrelevant, since it tells us nothing about the state of the auto industry then.

16. The answer is B, supports the conclusion. This is a tricky question. While at first it might seem to prove the conclusion, we can't be sure that the air bag legislation is responsible for the drop in automobile deaths. It's possible air bags came into popular use without the legislation, or with different legislation. There's no way we can be sure that it was the proposed legislation mandating the use of air bags that was responsible.

17. The answer is A. If, in June of 2009, the lobbyist received a bonus "for her work on the air bag legislation," we can be sure that the legislation passed. This proves the conclusion.

18. The answer is B. This is another tricky question. A three-fold stock increase would strongly suggest that the legislation had been passed, but it's possible that factors other than the air bag legislation caused the increase. Note that the stock is in "crash protection

equipment." Nowhere in the statement does it say air bags. Seat belts, motorcycle helmets, and collapsible bumpers are all crash protection equipment and could have contributed to the increase. This is just another reminder to read carefully because the questions are often designed to mislead you.

19. The answer is D. This would tend to weaken the conclusion because Joan is very fond of her mother and she would not want to upset her unnecessarily. It does not prove it, however, because if Joan strongly feels she is right, she probably wouldn't let her mother's opinion sway her. Choice E would also not be correct, because we cannot assume that Joan's mother's opinion is of so little importance to her as to be considered irrelevant.

20. The answer is E. The statement is irrelevant. We are told that Joan's income has doubled but we are not old why. The phrase "six months after the interview" can be misleading in that it leads us to assume that the increase and the interview are related. Her income could have doubled because she regained her popularity but it could also have come from stocks or some other business venture. Because we are not given any reason for her income doubling, it would be impossible to say whether or not this statement proves or disproves the conclusion. Choice E is the best choice of the five possible choices. One of the problems with promotional exams is that sometimes you need to select a choice you're not crazy about. In this case, "not having enough information to made a determination" would be the best choice. However, that's not an option, so you're forced to work with what you've got. On these exams it's sometimes like voting for President; you have to pick the "lesser of the two evils" or the least awful choice. In this case, the information is more irrelevant to the conclusion than it is anything else.

21. The answer is D, weakens the conclusion. We've been told that Joan's agent feels that she should apologize. If he is pleased with her interview, then it would tend to weaken the conclusion but not disprove it. We can't be sure that he hasn't had a change of heart, or that there weren't other parts of the interview he liked so much that they outweighed her unwillingness to apologize.

22. The answer is A. The conclusion states that Joan will donate $1 to the Cellulite Prevention League for every pound the actress loses. Joan's sister's financial report on the League's activities directly supports and proves the conclusion.

23. The answer is C, disproves the conclusion. If the magazine receives many letters commending Joan for her courage in apologizing, this directly contradicts the conclusion, which states that Joan didn't apologize.

24. The answer is B. It was stated in the passage that two of Joan's performances were cancelled after the controversy first occurred. The cancellation of another performance immediately after her interview was published would tend to support the conclusion that she refused to apologize. Because we can't be sure, however, that her performance wasn't cancelled for another reason, choice A would be incorrect.

25. The answer is E, as this information is irrelevant. Postponing the article an extra week does not affect Joan's decision or the public's reaction to it.

26. The answer is C. If 500 new employees are hired to handle the "increased paperwork created by the new tax on DVDs," this would directly contradict the conclusion, which states that the legislature defeated both bills. (They should all be this easy.)

27. The answer is B. The results of the study would support the conclusion. If implementing the legislation was going to be so costly, it is likely that the legislature would vote against it. Choice A is not the answer, however, because we can't be sure that the legislature didn't pass it anyway.

28. The answer is E. It's irrelevant to the conclusion that 80% of all those working in the entertainment industry own DVD recorders. Sometimes if you're not sure about these, it can help a lot to try and visualize the situation. Why would someone voting on this legislation care about this fact? It doesn't seem to be the kind of information that would make any difference or impact upon the conclusion.

29. The answer is B. The head of the law enforcement agency's statement that the legislation would be unenforceable would support the conclusion. It's possible that many legislators would question why they should bother to pass legislation that would be impossible to enforce. Choice A would be incorrect, however, because we can't be sure that the legislation wasn't passed in spite of his statement.

30. The answer is D. This would tend to weaken the conclusion because the prospect of several large companies going bankrupt would seem to be a good argument in favor of the legislation. The possible loss of jobs and businesses would be a good reason for some people to vote for the legislation. We can't be sure, however, that this would be a competing enough reason to ensure passage of the legislation so choice C is incorrect.

This concludes our section on the "Validity of Conclusion" type of questions. We hope these weren't too horrible for you. It's important to keep in mind <u>exactly</u> what you've been given and <u>exactly</u> what they want you to do with it. It's also necessary to remember that you may have to choose between two possible answers. In that case, you must choose the one that seems the best. Sometimes you may think there is no good answer. You will probably be right, but you can't let that upset you. Just choose the one you dislike the least.

We want to repeat that it is unlikely that this exact format will appear on the exam. The skills required to answer these questions, however, are the same as those you'll need for the exam so we suggest that you review this section before taking the actual exam.

31. The answer is C. This next set of questions requires you to "switch gears" slightly, and get used to different formats. In this type of question, you have to decide whether the conclusion is proved by the facts give, disproved by the facts given, or neither because note enough information has been provided. Fortunately, unlike the previous questions, you don't have to decide whether particular facts support or don't support the conclusion. This type of question is more straight forward, but the reasoning behind it is the same. We are told that the Bills have won two games less than the Patriots, and that the Patriots are in first place and the Bills are in second place. We are also told that there are two games left to play, and that they won't play each other again. The conclusion states that the Bills won the division. Is there anything in the four statements that would prove this? We have

no idea what the outcome of the last two games of the season was. The Bills and Patriots could have ended up tied at the end of the season, or the Bills could have lost both or one of their last games while the Patriots did the same. There might even be another team tied for first or second place with the Bills or Patriots. Since we don't know for sure, Choice A is incorrect. Choice B is trickier. It might seem at first glance that the best the Bills could do would be to tie the Patriots if the Patriots lost their last two games and the Bills won their last two games. But it would be too much to assume that there is no procedure for a tiebreaker that wouldn't give the Bills the division championship. Since we don't know what the rules are in the event of a tie (for example, what if a tie was decided on the results of what happened when the two teams had played each other, or on the best record in the division, or on most points scored?), we can't say for sure that it would be impossible for the Bills to win their division. For this reason, choice C is the answer, as we don't have enough information to prove or disprove the conclusion. This question looked more difficult than it actually was. It's important to disregard any factors outside of the actual question, and to focus only on what you've been given. In this case, as on all of these types of questions, what you know or don't know about a subject is actually irrelevant. It's best to concentrate only on the actual facts given.

32. The answer is A. The conclusion is proved by the facts given.

In this type of problem, it is usually best to pull as many facts as possible from the sentences and then put them into a simpler form. The phrasing and the order of exam questions are designed to be confusing so you need to restate things as clearly as possible by eliminating the extras.

Sentence I tells us that there are only two possible colors for eyes and two for hair. Looking at the other sentences we learn that eyes are either green or gold and that hair is either silver or purple. If half the beings with purple hair have golden eyes, then the other half must have green eyes since it is the only other eye color. Likewise, if one-third of those with silver hair have green eyes, the other two-thirds must have golden eyes.

This information makes it clear that there are more golden-eyed beings on Zeinon than green-eyed ones. It doesn't matter that we don't know exactly how many are actually living on the planet. The number of those with gold eyes (1/2 plus 2/3) will always be greater than the number of those with green eyes (1/2 plus 1/3), no matter what the actual figures might be. Sentence III is totally irrelevant because even if there were more silver-haired inhabitants it would not affect the conclusion.

33. The answer is C. The conclusion is neither proved nor disproved by the facts because we don't know how many miles Bethany is from Amoranth.

With this type of question, if you're not sure how to approach it, you can always substitute in a range of "real numbers" to see what the result would be. If they were 200 miles apart, Joe's Truck Rental would be cheaper because they would charge a total of $160 while National Movers would charge $175.

Joe's - $100 plus .30 x 200 (or $60) = $160
National - $150 plus .25 x 100 (or $25) = $175

If the towns were 600 miles apart, however, National Movers would be cheaper. The cost of renting from National would be $275 compared to the $280 charged by Joe's Trucking.

Joe's - $100 plus .30 x 600 (or $180) = $280
National - $150 plus .25 x 500 (or $125) = $275

34. The answer is B. We've varied the format once more, but the reasoning is similar. This is a tedious question that is more like a math question, but we wanted to give you some practice with this type, just in case. You won't be able to do this question if you've forgotten how to do percents. Many exams require this knowledge, so if you feel you need a review we suggest you read Booklets 1, 2 or 3 in this series.

The only way to attack this problem is to go through each choice until you find the one that is correct. Choice A states that Plainfield, Smallville, and Granton are cities. Let's begin with Plainfield. The passage states that in 1990 Plainfield had a population of 12,000, and that it grew 10% between 1990 and 2000, and another 20% between 2000 and 2010. Ten percent of 12,000 is 1200 (12,000 x .10 = 1200). Therefore, the population grew from 12,000 in 1990 to 12,000 + 1200 between 1990 and 2000. At the time of the 2000 Census, Plainfield's population was 13,200. It then grew another 20% between 2000 and 2010, so, 13,200 x .20 = 2640. 13,200 plus the additional increase of 2640 would make the population of Plainfield 15,840. This would qualify it as a city, since its population is over 15,000. Since a change upward in the population of a municipality is re-classified immediately, Plainfield would have become a city right away. So far, statement A is true. The passage states that Smallville's population has not changed significantly in the last twenty years. Since Smallville's population was 20,283, Smallville would still be a city. Granton had a population of 25,000 (what a coincidence that so any of these places have such nice, even numbers) in 1980. The population has decreased 25% in each ten year period since that time. So from 1980 to 1990, the population decreased 25%. 25,000 x .25 = 6,250. 25,000 minus 6,250 = 18,750. So the population of Granton in 1990 would have been 18,750. (Or, you could have saved a step and multiplied 25,000 by .75 to get 18,750.) The population from 1990 to 2000 decreased an additional 25%. So: 18,750 x .25 = 4,687.50. 18,750 minus 4,687.50 = 14,062.50. Or: 18,750 x .75 = 14,062.50. (Don't let the fact that a half of a person is involved confuse you; these are exam questions, not real life.) From 2000 to 2010 the population decreased an additional 25%. This would mean that Granton's population was below 15,000 for more than ten years, so it's status as a city would have changed to that of a town, which would make choice A incorrect.

Choice B states that Smallville is a city and Granton is a town, which we know to be true from the information above. Choice B is correct so far. We next need to determine if Ellenville is a village. Ellenville had a population of 4,283 in 1980, and increased 5% in each ten year period since 1980. 4,283 x .05 = 214.15. 4,283 plus 214.15 = 4,497.15, so Ellenville's population from 1980 to 1990 increased to 4,497.15. (Or: 4,283 x 1.05 – 4,497.15.) From 1990 to 2000 Ellenville's population increased another 5%: 4,497.15 x .05 = 224.86. 4,497.15 plus 224.86 = 4,772.01 (or: 4,497.15 x 1.05 = 4,722.01.) From 2000 to 2010, Ellenville's population increased another 5%: 4,722.01 x .05 = 236.10. 4,722.01 plus 236.10 = 4,958.11. (Or: 4,722.01 x 1.05 = 4,958.11.).

Ellenville's population is still under 5,000 in 2010, so it would continue to be classified as a village. Since all three statements in choice B are true, choice B must be the answer. However, we'll go through the other choices. Choice C states that Springdale is a town. The passage tells us that the population of Springdale doubled from 1990 to 2000, and increased 25% from 2000 to 2010. It doesn't give us any actual population figures, however, so it's impossible to know what the population of Springdale is, making choice C incorrect. Choice C also states that Granton is a town, which is true, and that Ellenville is a town, which is false (from choice B we know it's a village). Choice D states that Plainfield and Smallville are cities, which is information we already know is true, and that Ellenville is a town. Since Ellenville is a village, choice D is also incorrect.

This was a lot of work for just one question and we doubt you'll get one like this on this section of the exam, but we included it just in case. On an exam, you can always put a check mark next to a question like this and come back to it later, if you feel you're pressed for time and cold spend your time more productively on other, less time-consuming problems.

35. The answer is B. This question requires very careful reading. It's best to break the conclusion down into smaller parts in order to solve the problem. The first half of the conclusion states that the average person in the 20-29 age group (Group A) drinks less tea daily than the average person in the 40-50 age group (Group C). The average person in Group A drinks 2.1 cups of tea daily, while the average person in Group C drinks 2.6 cups of tea daily. Since 2.1 is less than 2.6, the conclusion is correct so far. The second half of the conclusion states that the average person in Group A drinks more coffee daily than the average person in the 30-39 age group (Group B) drinks cola. The average person in Group A drinks 1.8 cups of coffee daily, while the average person in Group B drinks 1.9 glasses of cola. This disproves the conclusion, which states that the average person in Group A drinks more coffee daily than the average person in Group B drinks cola.

36. The answer is C. The easiest way to approach a problem that deals with the relationship between a number of different people or things is to set up a diagram. This type of problem is usually too confusing to do in your head. For this particular problem, the "diagram" could be a line, one end of which would be labeled tall and the other end labeled short. Then, taking one sentence at a time, place the people on the line to see where they fall in relation to one another.

The diagram of the first sentence would look like this:

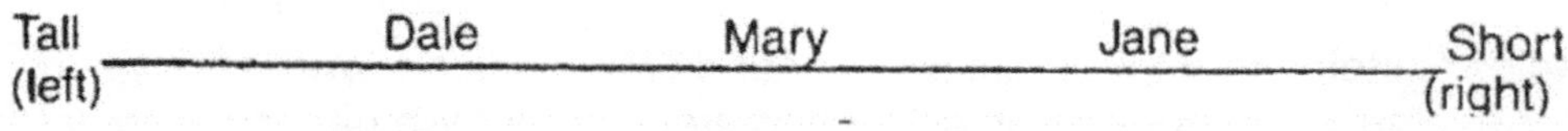

Mary is taller than Jane but shorter than Dale, so she would fall somewhere between the two of them. We have placed tall on the left and labeled it left just to make the explanation easier. You could just as easily have reversed the position.

The second sentence places Fred somewhere to the left of Mary because he is taller than she is. Steven would be to the left of Fred for the same reason. At this point we don't know whether Steven and Fred are taller or shorter than Dale. The new diagram would look like this:

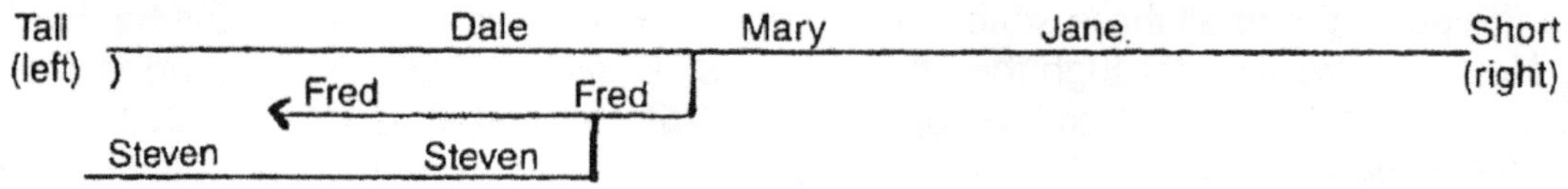

The third sentence introduces Elizabeth, presenting a new problem. Elizabeth can be anywhere to the right of Dale. Don't make the mistake of assuming she falls between Dale and Mary. At this point we don't know where she fits in relation to Mary, Jane, or even Fred.

We do get information about Steven, however. He is taller than Dale so he would be to the left of Dale. Since he is also taller than Fred (see sentence II), we know that Steven is the tallest person thus far. The diagram would now look like this:

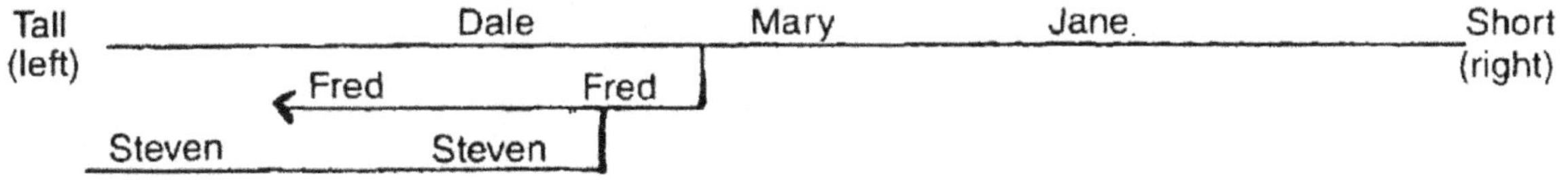

Fred's height is somewhere between Steven and Mary, Elizabeth's anywhere between Dale and the end of the line.

The fourth sentence tells us where Elizabeth stands, in relation to Fred and the others in the problem. The fact that she is taller than Mary means she is also taller than Jane. The final diagram would look like this:

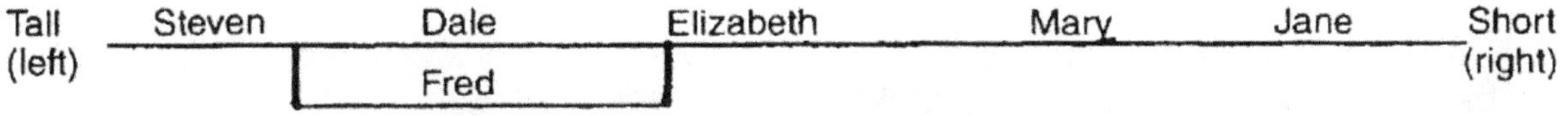

We still don't know whether Dale or Fred is taller, however. Therefore, the conclusion that Dale is taller than Fred can't be proved. It also can't be disproved because we don't know for sure that he isn't. The answer has to be choice C, as the conclusion can't be proved or disproved.

37. The answer is A. This is another problem that is easiest for most people if they make a diagram. Sentence I states that Main Street is between Spring Street and Glenn Blvd. At this point we don't know if they are next to each other or if they are separated by a number of streets. Therefore, you should leave space between streets as you plot your first diagram.

The order of the streets could go either:

Spring St. Main St. Glenn Blvd.	or	Glenn Blvd. Main St. Spring St.

Sentence II states that Hawley Street is one block south of Spring Street and 3 blocks north of Main Street. Because most people think in terms of north as above and south as below and because it was stated that Hawley is one block south of Spring Street and three blocks north of Main Street, the next diagram could look like this:

18 (#1)

Spring
Hawley
______
______
Main
Glenn

The third sentence states that Glenn Street is five blocks south of Elm and four blocks south of Main. It could look like this:

Spring
Hawley
______
Elm
Main
____
____
____
Glenn

The conclusion states that Elm Street is between Hawley Avenue and Glenn Blvd. From the above diagram, we can see that this is the case.

38. The answer is B. For most people, the best way to do this problem is to draw a diagram, plotting the course of both trains. Sentence I states that Train A leaves Hampshire at 5:50 A.M. and reaches New London at 6:42. Your first diagram might look like this:

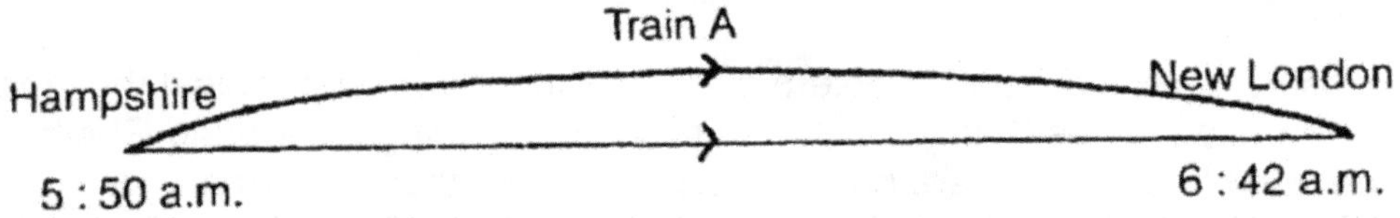

Sentence II states that the train leaves New London at 7:00 a.m. and arrives in Kellogsville at 8:42 a.m. The diagram might now look like this:

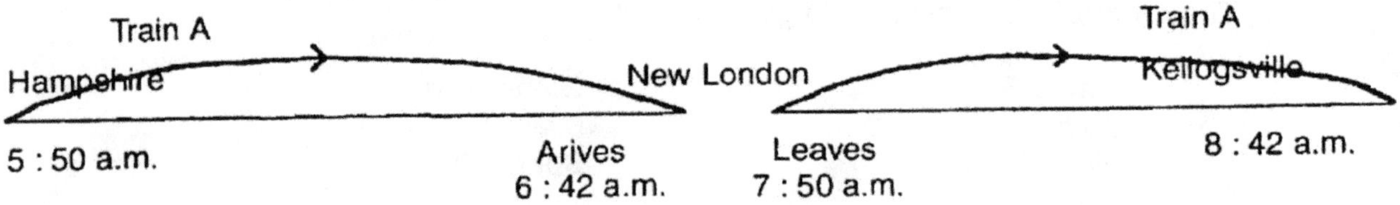

Sentence III gives us the rest of the information that must be included in the diagram. It introduces Train B, which moves in the opposite direction, leaving Kellogsville at 8:00 a.m. and arriving at Hampshire at 10:42 a.m. The final diagram might look like this:

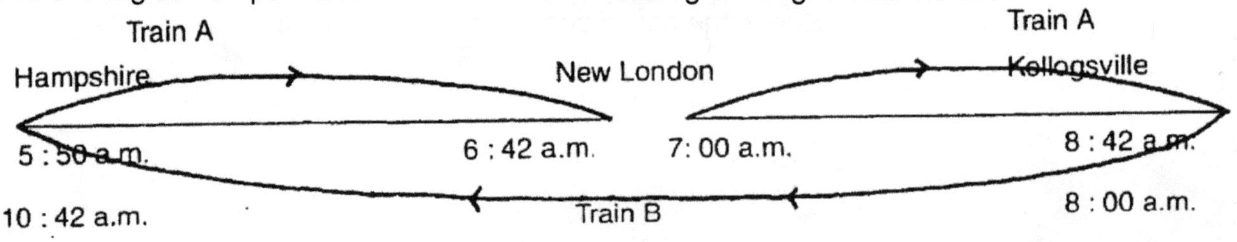

19 (#1)

As you can see from the diagram, the routes of the two trains will overlap somewhere between Kellogsville and New London. If you read sentence IV quickly and assumed that that was the section with only one track, you probably would have assumed that there would have had to be a collision. Sentence IV states, however, that there is only one railroad track between New London and Hampshire. That is the only section, then, where the two trains could collide. By the time Train B gets to that section, however, Train A will have passed it. The two trains will pass each other somewhere between New London and Kellogsville, not New London and Hampshire.

PRINCIPLES AND PRACTICES, OF ADMINISTRATION, SUPERVISION AND MANAGEMENT

TABLE OF CONTENTS

PRINCIPLES AND PRACTICES, OF ADMINISTRATION, SUPERVISION AND MANAGEMENT

Most people are inclined to think of administration as something that only a few persons are responsible for in a large organization. Perhaps this is true if you are thinking of Administration with a capital *A*, but administration with a lower case *a* is a responsibility of supervisors at all levels each working day.

All of us feel we are pretty good supervisors and that we do a good job of administering the workings of our agency. By and large, this is true, but every so often it is good to check up on ourselves. Checklists appear from time to time in various publications which psychologists say tell whether or not a person will make a good wife, husband, doctor, lawyer, or supervisor.

The following questions are an excellent checklist to test yourself as a supervisor and administrator.

Remember, Administration gives direction and points the way but administration carries the ideas to fruition. Each is dependent on the other for its success. Remember, too, that no unit is too small for these departmental functions to be carried out. These statements apply equally as well to the Chief Librarian as to the Department Head with but one or two persons to supervise.

GENERAL ADMINISTRATION: General Responsibilities of Supervisors

1. Have I prepared written statements of functions, activities, and duties for my organizational unit?

2. Have I prepared procedural guides for operating activities?

3. Have I established clearly in writing, lines of authority and responsibility for my organizational unit?

4. Do I make recommendations for improvements in organization, policies, administrative and operating routines and procedures, including simplification of work and elimination of non-essential operations?

5. Have I designated and trained an understudy to function in my absence?

6. Do I supervise and train personnel within the unit to effectively perform their assignments?

7. Do I assign personnel and distribute work on such a basis as to carry out the organizational unit's assignment or mission in the most effective and efficient manner?

8. Have I established administrative controls by:

    a. Fixing responsibility and accountability on all supervisors under my direction for the proper performance of their functions and duties.

b. Preparations and submitting periodic work load and progress reports covering the operations of the unit to my immediate superior.

c. Analysis and evaluation of such reports received from subordinate units.

d. Submission of significant developments and problems arising within the organizational unit to my immediate superior.

e. Conducting conferences, inspections, etc., as to the status and efficiency of unit operations.

9. Do I maintain an adequate and competent working force?

10. Have I fostered good employee-department relations, seeing that established rules, regulations, and instructions are being carried out properly?

11. Do I collaborate and consult with other organizational units performing related functions to insure harmonious and efficient working relationships?

12. Do I maintain liaison through prescribed channels with city departments and other governmental agencies concerned with the activities of the unit?

13. Do I maintain contact with and keep abreast of the latest developments and techniques of administration (professional societies, groups, periodicals, etc.) as to their applicability to the activities of the unit?

14. Do I communicate with superiors and subordinates through prescribed organizational channels?

15. Do I notify superiors and subordinates in instances where bypassing is necessary as soon thereafter as practicable?

16. Do I keep my superior informed of significant developments and problems?

SEVEN BASIC FUNCTIONS OF THE SUPERVISOR

I. PLANNING
This means working out goals and means to obtain goals. What needs to be done, who will do it, how, when, and where it is to be done.

SEVEN STEPS IN PLANNING

A. Define job or problem clearly.
B. Consider priority of job.
C. Consider time-limit—starting and completing.
D. Consider minimum distraction to, or interference with, other activities.
E. Consider and provide for contingencies—possible emergencies.
F. Break job down into components.

G. Consider the 5 W's and H:
WHY..........is it necessary to do the job? (Is the purpose clearly defined?)
WHAT........needs to be done to accomplish the defined purpose?
.........is needed to do the job? (Money, materials, etc.)
WHO..........is needed to do the job?
..........will have responsibilities?
WHERE......is the work to be done?
WHEN........is the job to begin and end? (Schedules, etc.)
HOW..........is the job to bed done? (Methods, controls, records, etc.)

II. ORGANIZING

This means dividing up the work, establishing clear lines of responsibility and authority and coordinating efforts to get the job done.

III. STAFFING

The whole personnel function of bringing in and training staff, getting the right man and fitting him to the right job—the job to which he is best suited.

In the normal situation, the supervisor's responsibility regarding staffing normally includes providing accurate job descriptions, that is, duties of the jobs, requirements, education and experience, skills, physical, etc.; assigning the work for maximum use of skills; and proper utilization of the probationary period to weed out unsatisfactory employees.

IV. DIRECTING

Providing the necessary leadership to the group supervised. Important work gets done to the supervisor's satisfaction.

V. COORDINATING

The all-important duty of inter-relating the various parts of the work.
The supervisor is also responsible for controlling the coordinated activities. This means measuring performance according to a time schedule and setting quotas to see that the goals previously set are being reached. Reports from workers should be analyzed, evaluated, and made part of all future plans.

VI. REPORTING

This means proper and effective communication to your superiors, subordinates, and your peers (in definition of the job of the supervisor). Reports should be read and information contained therein should be used, not be filed away and forgotten. Reports should be written in such a way that the desired action recommended by the report is forthcoming.

VII. BUDGETING
This means controlling current costs and forecasting future costs. This forecast is based on past experience, future plans and programs, as well as current costs.

You will note that these seven functions can fall under three topics:

Planning) Make a plan Organizing)	Staffing) Directing) Get things done Controlling)	Reporting) Watch it work Budgeting)

PLANNING TO MEET MANAGEMENT GOALS

I. WHAT IS PLANNING?

A. Thinking a job through before new work is done to determine the best way to do it
B. A method of doing something
C. Ways and means for achieving set goals
D. A means of enabling a supervisor to deliver with a minimum of effort, all details involved in coordinating his work

II. WHO SHOULD MAKE PLANS?

Everybody!
All levels of supervision must plan work. (Top management, heads of divisions or bureaus, first line supervisors, and individual employees.) The higher the level, the more planning required.

III. WHAT ARE THE RESULTS OF POOR PLANNING?

A. Failure to meet deadline
B. Low employee morale
C. Lack of job coordination
D. Overtime is frequently necessary
E. Excessive cost, waste of material and manhours

IV. PRINCIPLES OF PLANNING

A. Getting a clear picture of your objectives. What exactly are you trying to accomplish?
B. Plan the whole job, then the parts, in proper sequence.
C. Delegate the planning of details to those responsible for executing them.
D. Make your plan flexible.
E. Coordinate your plan with the plans of others so that the work may be processed with a minimum of delay.
F. Sell your plan before you execute it.
G. Sell your plan to your superior, subordinate, in order to gain maximum participation and coordination.
H. Your plan should take precedence. Use knowledge and skills that others have brought to a similar job.
I. Your plan should take account of future contingencies; allow for future expansion.
J. Plans should include minor details. Leave nothing to chance that can be anticipated.
K. Your plan should be simple and provide standards and controls. Establish quality and quantity standards and set a standard method of doing the job. The controls will indicate whether the job is proceeding according to plan.
L. Consider possible bottlenecks, breakdowns, or other difficulties that are likely to arise.

V. Q. WHAT ARE THE YARDSTICKS BY WHICH PLANNING SHOULD BE MEASURED?
A. Any plan should:
—Clearly state a definite course of action to be followed and goal to be achieved, with consideration for emergencies.
— Be realistic and practical.
— State what's to be done, when it's to be done, where, how, and by whom.
— Establish the most efficient sequence of operating steps so that more is accomplished in less time, with the least effort, and with the best quality results.
— Assure meeting deliveries without delays.
— Establish the standard by which performance is to be judged.

Q. WHAT KINDS OF PLANS DOES EFFECTIVE SUPERVISION REQUIRE?
A. Plans should cover such factors as:
— Manpower: right number of properly trained employees on the job
— Materials: adequate supply of the right materials and supplies
— Machines: full utilization of machines and equipment, with proper maintenance
— Methods: most efficient handling of operations
— Deliveries: making deliveries on time
— Tools: sufficient well-conditioned tools
— Layout: most effective use of space
— Reports: maintaining proper records and reports
— Supervision: planning work for employees and organizing supervisor's own time

MANAGEMENT PRINCIPLES

I. MANAGEMENT
Q. What do we mean by management?
A. Getting work done through others.

Management could also be defined as planning, directing, and controlling the operations of a bureau or division so that all factors will function properly and all persons cooperate efficiently for a common objective.

II. MANAGEMENT PRINCIPLES

A. There should be a hierarchy—wherein authority and responsibility run upward and downward through several levels—with a broad base at the bottom and a single head at the top.

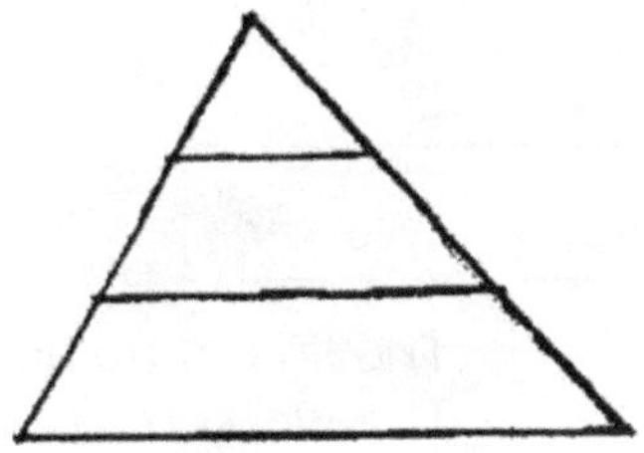

B. Each and every unit or person in the organization should be answerable ultimately to the manager at the apex. In other words, *The buck stops here!*

C. Every necessary function involved in the bureau's objectives is assigned to a unit in that bureau.

D. Responsibilities assigned to a unit are specifically clear-cut and understood.

E. Consistent methods of organizational structure should be applied at each level of the organization.

F. Each member of the bureau from top to bottom knows: to whom he reports and who reports to him.

G. No member of one bureau reports to more than one supervisor. No dual functions.

H. Responsibility for a function is matched by authority necessary to perform that function. Weight of authority.

I. Individuals or units reporting to a supervisor do not exceed the number which can be feasibly and effectively coordinated and directed. Concept of *span of control.*

J. Channels of command (management) are not violated by staff units, although there should be staff services to facilitate and coordinate management functions.

K. Authority and responsibility should be decentralized to units and individuals who are responsible for the actual performance of operations.
Welfare – down to Welfare Centers
Hospitals – down to local hospitals

L. Management should exercise control through attention to policy problems of exceptional performance, rather than through review of routine actions of subordinates.

M. Organizations should never be permitted to grow so elaborate as to hinder work accomplishments.

III. ORGANIZATION STRUCTURE

Types of Organizations
The purest form is a leader and a few followers, such as:

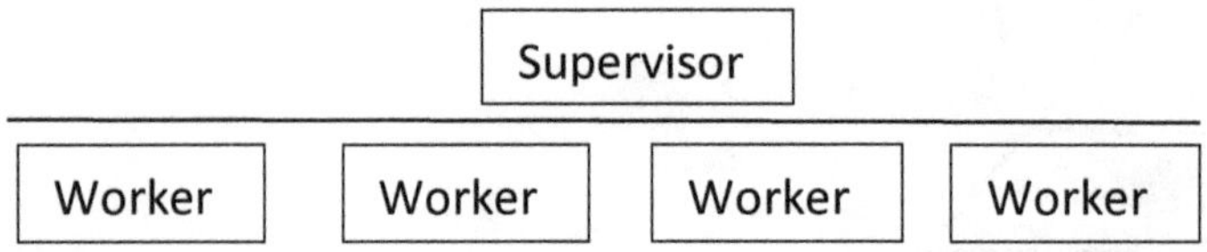

(Refer to organization chart) from supervisor to workers.

The line of authority is direct, The workers know exactly where they stand in relation to their boss, to whom they report for instructions and direction.

Unfortunately, in our present complex society, few organizations are similar to this example of a pure line organization. In this era of specialization, other people are often needed in the simplest of organizations. These specialists are known as staff. The sole purpose for their existence (staff) is to assist, advise, suggest, help or counsel line organizations. Staff has no authority to direct line people—nor do they give them direct instructions.

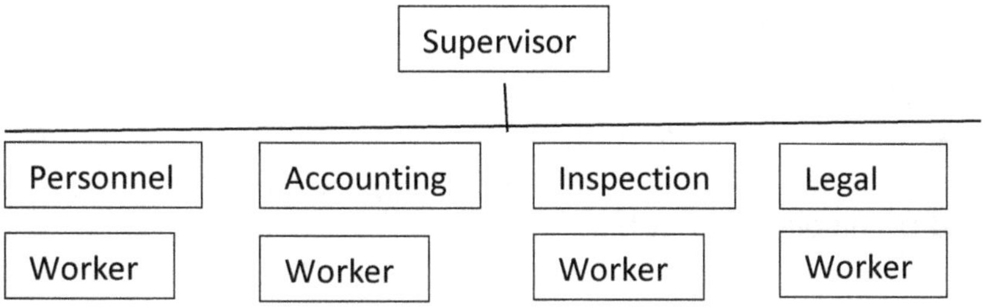

Line Functions

1. Directs
2. Orders
3. Responsibility for carrying out activities from beginning to end
4. Follows chain of command
5. Is identified with what it does
6. Decides when and how to use staff advice
7. Line executes

Staff Functions

1. Advises
2. Persuades and sells
3. Staff studies, reports, recommends but does not carry out
4. May advise across department lines
5. May find its ideas identified with others
6. Has to persuade line to want its advice
7. Staff: Conducts studies and research. Provides advice and instructions in technical matters. Serves as technical specialist to render specific services.

Types and Functions of Organization Charts

An organization chart is a picture of the arrangement and inter-relationship of the subdivisions of an organization.

A. Types of Charts:
   1. Structural: basic relationships only
   2. Functional: includes functions or duties
   3. Personnel: positions, salaries, status, etc.
   4. Process Chart: work performed
   5. Gantt Chart: actual performance against planned
   5. Flow Chart: flow and distribution of work

B. Functions of Charts:
   1. Assist in management planning and control
   2. Indicate duplication of functions
   3. Indicate incorrect stressing of functions
   4. Indicate neglect of important functions
   5. Correct unclear authority
   6. Establish proper span of control

C. Limitations of Charts:
   1. Seldom maintained on current basis
   2. Chart is oversimplified
   3. Human factors cannot adequately be charted

D. Organization Charts should be:
   1. Simple
   2. Symmetrical
   3. Indicate authority
   4. Line and staff relationship differentiated
   5. Chart should be dated and bear signature of approving officer
   6. Chart should be displayed, not hidden

ORGANIZATION

There are four basic principles of organization:
1. Unity of command
2. Span of control
3. Uniformity of assignment
4. Assignment of responsibility and delegation of authority

I. UNITY OF COMMAND

Unity of command means that each person in the organization should receive orders from one, and only one, supervisor. When a person has to take orders from two or more people, (a) the orders may be in conflict and the employee is upset because he does not know which he should obey, or (b) different orders may reach him at the same time and he does not know which he should carry out first.

Equally as bad as having two bosses is the situation where the supervisor is bypassed. Let us suppose you are a supervisor whose boss bypasses you (deals directly with people reporting to you). To the worker, it is the same as having two bosses; but to you, the supervisor, it is equally serious. Bypassing on the part of your boss will undermine your authority, and the people under you will begin looking to your boss for decisions and even for routine orders.

You can prevent bypassing by telling the people you supervise that if anyone tries to give them orders, they should direct that person to you.

II. SPAN OF CONTROL

Span of control on a given level involves:
A. The number of people being supervised
B. The distance
C The time involved in supervising the people. (One supervisor cannot supervise too many workers effectively.)

Span of control means that a supervisor has the right number (not too many and not too few) of subordinates that he can supervise well.

III. UNIFORMITY OF ASSIGNMENT

In assigning work, you as the supervisor should assign to each person jobs that are similar in nature. An employee who is assigned too many different types of jobs will waste time in going from one kind of work to another. It takes time for him to get to top production in one kind of task and, before he does so, he has to start on another.
When you assign work to people, remember that:

A. Job duties should be definite. Make it clear from the beginning what they are to do, how they are to do it, and why they are to do it. Let them know how much they are expected to do and how well they are expected to do it.
B. Check your assignments to be certain that there are no workers with too many unrelated duties, and that no two people have been given overlapping responsibilities. Your aim should be to have every task assigned to a specific person with the work fairly distributed and with each person doing his part.

IV. ASSIGNMENT OF RESPONSIBILITY AND DELEGATION OF AUTHORITY

A supervisor cannot delegate his final responsibility for the work of his department. The experienced supervisor knows that he gets his work done through people. He can't do it all himself. So he must assign the work and the responsibility for the work to his employees. Then they must be given the authority to carry out their responsibilities.

By assigning responsibility and delegating authority to carry out the responsibility, the supervisor builds in his workers initiative, resourcefulness, enthusiasm, and interest in their work. He is treating them as responsible adults. They can find satisfaction in their work, and they will respect the supervisor and be loyal to the supervisor.

PRINCIPLES OF ORGANIZATION

I. DEFINITION

Organization is the method of dividing up the work to provide the best channels for coordinated effort to get the agency's mission accomplished.

II. PURPOSE OF ORGANIZATION

A. To enable each employee within the organization to clearly know his responsibilities and relationships to his fellow employees and to organizational units
B. To avoid conflicts of authority and overlapping of jurisdiction.
C. To ensure teamwork.

III. BASIC CONSIDERATIONS IIN ORGANIZATIONAL PLANNING

A. The basic plans and objectives of the agency should be determined, and the organizational structure should be adapted to carry out effectively such plans and objectives.
B. The organization should be built around the major functions of the agency and not individuals or groups of individuals.

C. The organization should be sufficiently flexible to meet new and changing conditions which may be brought about from within or outside the department.
D. The organizational structure should be as simple as possible and the number of organizational units kept at a minimum.
E. The number of levels of authority should be kept at a minimum. Each additional management level lengthens the chain of authority and responsibility and increases the time for instructions to be distributed to operating levels and for decisions to be obtained from higher authority.
F. The form of organization should permit each executive to exercise maximum initiative within the limits of delegated authority.

IV. BASES FOR ORGANIZATION

A. Purpose (Examples: education, police, sanitation)
B. Process (Examples: accounting, legal, purchasing)
C. Clientele (Examples: welfare, parks, veteran)
D. Geographic (Examples: borough offices, precincts, libraries)

V. ASSIGNMENTS OF FUNCTIONS

A. Every function of the agency should be assigned to a specific organizational unit. Under normal circumstances, no single function should be assigned to more than one organizational unit.
B. There should be no overlapping, duplication, or conflict between organizational elements.
C. Line functions should be separated from staff functions, and proper emphasis should be placed on staff activities.
D. Functions which are closely related or similar should normally be assigned to a single organizational unit.
E. Functions should be properly distributed to promote balance, and to avoid overemphasis of less important functions and underemphasis of more essential functions.

VI. DELEGATION OF AUTHORITY AND RESPONSIBILITY

A. Responsibilities assigned to a specific individual or organizational unit should carry corresponding authority, and all statements of authority or limitations thereof should be as specific as possible.
B. Authority and responsibility for action should be decentralized to organizational units and individuals responsible for actual performance to the greatest extent possible, without relaxing necessary control over policy or the standardization of procedures. Delegation of authority will be consistent with decentralization of responsibility but such delegation will not divest an executive in higher authority of his overall responsibility.
C. The heads of organizational units should concern themselves with important matters and should delegate to the maximum extent details and routines performed in the ordinary course of business.
D. All responsibilities, authorities, and relationships should be stated in simple language to avoid misinterpretation.
E. Each individual or organizational unit charged with a specific responsibility will be held responsible for results.

VII. EMPLOYEE RELATIONSHIPS

A. The employees reporting to one executive should not exceed the number which can be effectively directed and coordinated. The number will depend largely upon the scope and extent of the responsibilities of the subordinates.
B. No person should report to more than one supervisor. Every supervisor should know who reports to him, and every employee should know to whom he reports. Channels of authority and responsibility should not be violated by staff units.
C. Relationships between organizational units within the agency and with outside organizations and associations should be clearly stated and thoroughly understood to avoid misunderstanding.

DELEGATING

I. WHAT IS DELEGATING?
Delegating is assigning a job to an employee, giving him the authority to get that job done, and giving him the responsibility for seeing to it that the job is done.

A. What To Delegate
   1. Routine details
   2. Jobs which may be necessary and take a lot of time, but do not have to be done by the supervisor personally (preparing reports, attending meetings, etc.)
   3. Routine decision-making (making decisions which do not require the supervisor's personal attention)

B. What Not To Delegate
   1. Job details which are *executive functions* (setting goals, organizing employees into a good team, analyzing results so as to plan for the future)
   2. Disciplinary power (handling grievances, preparing service ratings, reprimands, etc.)
   3. Decision-making which involves large numbers of employees or other bureaus and departments
   4. Final and complete responsibility for the job done by the unit being supervised

C. Why Delegate?
   1. To strengthen the organization by developing a greater number of skilled employees
   2. To improve the employee's performance by giving him the chance to learn more about the job, handle some responsibility, and become more interested in getting the job done
   3. To improve a supervisor's performance by relieving him of routine jobs and giving him more time for *executive functions* (planning, organizing, controlling, etc.) which cannot be delegated

II. TO WHOM TO DELEGATE
People with abilities not being used. Selection should be based on ability, not on favoritism.

REPORTS

I. DEFINITION

A report is an orderly presentation of factual information directed to a specific reader for a specific purpose

II. PURPOSE

The general purpose of a report is to bring to the reader useful and factual information about a condition or a problem. Some specific purposes of a report may be:

A. To enable the reader to appraise the efficiency or effectiveness of a person or an operation
B. To provide a basis for establishing standards
C. To reflect the results of expenditures of time, effort, and money
D. To provide a basis for developing or altering programs

III. TYPES

A. Information Report: Contains facts arranged in sequence
B. Summary (Examination) Report: Contains facts plus an analysis or discussion of the significance of the facts. Analysis may give advantages and disadvantages or give qualitative and quantitative comparisons
C. Recommendation Report: Contains facts, analysis, and conclusion logically drawn from the facts and analysis, plus a recommendation based upon the facts, analysis, and conclusions

IV. FACTORS TO CONSIDER BEFORE WRITING REPORT

A. Why write the report?: The purpose of the report should be clearly defined.
B. Who will read the report?: What level of language should be used? Will the reader understand professional or technical language?
C. What should be said?: What does the reader need or want to know about the subject?
D. How should it be said?: Should the subject be presented tactfully? Convincingly? In a stimulating manner?

V. PREPARATORY STEPS

A. Assemble the facts: Find out who, why, what, where, when, and how.
B. Organize the facts: Eliminate unnecessary information
C. Prepare an outline: Check for orderliness, logical sequence
D. Prepare a draft: Check for correctness, clearness, completeness, conciseness, and tone
E. Prepare it in final form: Check for grammar, punctuation, appearance

VI. OUTLINE FOR A RECOMMENDATION REPORT

Is the report:

A. Correct in information, grammar, and tone?
B. Clear?
C. Complete?

D. Concise?
E. Timely?
F. Worth its cost?

Will the report accomplish its purpose?

MANAGEMENT CONTROLS

I. CONTROL
What is control? What is controlled? Who controls?

The essence of control is action which adjusts operations to predetermined standards, and its basis is information in the hands of managers. Control is checking to determine whether plans are being observed and suitable progress toward stated objectives is being made, and action is taken, if necessary, to correct deviations.

We have a ready-made model for this concept of control in the automatic systems which are widely used for process control in the chemical land petroleum industries. A process control system works this way. Suppose, for example, it is desired to maintain a constant rate of flow of oil through a pipe at a predetermined or set-point value. A signal, whose strength represents the rate of flow, can be produced in a measuring device and transmitted to a control mechanism. The control mechanism, when it detects any deviation of the actual from the set-point signal, will reposition the value regulating flow rate.

II. BASIS FOR CONTROL

A process control mechanism thus acts to adjust operations to predetermined standards and does so on the basis of information it receives. In a parallel way, information reaching a manager gives him the opportunity for corrective action and is his basis for control. He cannot exercise control without such information, and he cannot do a complete job of managing without controlling.

III. POLICY

What is policy?

Policy is simply a statement of an organization's intention to act in certain ways when specified types of circumstances arise. It represents a general decision, predetermined and expressed as a principle or rule, establishing a normal pattern of conduct for dealing with given types of business events—usually recurrent. A statement is therefore useful in economizing the time of managers and in assisting them to discharge their responsibilities equitably and consistently.

Policy is not a means of control, but policy does generate the need for control.

Adherence to policies is not guaranteed nor can it be taken on faith. It has to be verified. Without verification, there is no basis for control. Policy and procedures, although closely related and interdependent to a certain extent, are not synonymous. A policy may be adopted, for example, to maintain a materials inventory not to exceed one million dollars.

A procedure for inventory control could interpret that policy and convert it into methods for keeping within that limit, with consideration, too, of possible but foreseeable expedient deviation.

IV. PROCEDURE

What is procedure?

A procedure specifically prescribes:
A. What work is to be performed by the various participants
B. Who are the respective participants
C. When and where the various steps in the different processes are to be performed
D. The sequence of operations that will insure uniform handling of recurring transactions
E. The paper that is involved, its origin, transition, and disposition

Necessary appurtenances to a procedure are:
A. Detailed organizational chart
B. Flow charts
C. Exhibits of forms, all presented in close proximity to the text of the procedure

V. BASIS OF CONTROL – INFORMATION IN THE HANDS OF MANAGERS

If the basis of control is information in the hands of managers, then reporting is elevated to a level of very considerable importance.

Types of reporting may include:
A. Special reports and routine reports
B. Written, oral, and graphic reports
C. Staff meetings
D. Conferences
E. Television screens
F. Non-receipt of information, as where management is by exception
G. Any other means whereby information is transmitted to a manager as a basis for control action

FRAMEWORK OF MANAGEMENT

I. ELEMENTS

A. Policy: It has to be verified, controlled.

B. Organization is part of the giving of an assignment. The organizational chart gives to each individual in his title, a first approximation of the nature of his assignment and orients him as being accountable to a certain individual. Organization is not in a true sense a means of control. Control is checking to ascertain whether the assignment is executed as intended and acting on the basis of that information.

C. Budgets perform three functions:
   1. They present the objectives, plans, and programs of the organization in financial terms.

2. They report the progress of actual performance against these predetermined objectives, plans, and programs.
3. Like organizational charts, delegations of authority, procedures, and job descriptions, they define the assignments which have flowed from the Chief Executive. Budgets are a means of control in the respect that they report progress of actual performance against the program. They provide information which enables managers to take action directed toward bringing actual results into conformity with the program.

D. Internal Check provides in practice for the principle that the same person should not have responsibility for all phases of a transaction. This makes it clearly an aspect of organization rather than of control. Internal Check is static, or built-in.

E. Plans, Programs, Objectives
People must know what they are trying to do. Objectives fulfill this need. Without them, people may work industriously and yet, working aimlessly, accomplish little. Plans and Programs complement Objectives, since they propose how and according to what time schedule the objectives are to be reached.

F. Delegations of Authority
Among the ways we have for supplementing the titles and lines of authority of an organizational chart are delegations of authority. Delegations of authority clarify the extent of authority of individuals and in that way serve to define assignments. That they are not means of control is apparent from the very fact that wherever there has been a delegation of authority, the need for control increases. This could hardly be expected to happen if delegations of authority were themselves means of control.

II. MANAGER'S RESPONSIBILITY

Control becomes necessary whenever a manager delegates authority to a subordinate because he cannot delegate and then simply sit back and forget4 about it. A manager's accountability to his own superior has not diminished one whit as a result of delegating part of his authority to a subordinate. The manager must exercise control over actions taken under the authority so delegated. That means checking serves as a basis for possible corrective action.

Objectives, plans, programs, organizational charts, and other elements of the managerial system are not fruitfully regarded as either controls or means of control. They are pre-established standards or models of performance to which operations are adjusted by the exercise of management control. These standards or models of performance are dynamic in character for they are constantly altered, modified, or revised. Policies, organizational set-up, procedures, delegations, etc. are constantly altered but, like objectives and plans, they remain in force until they are either abandoned or revised. All of the elements (or standards or models of performance), objectives, plans, and programs, policies, organization, etc. can be regarded as a *framework of management*.

III. CONTROL TECHNIQUES

Examples of control techniques:

A. Compare against established standards
B. Compare with a similar operation
C. Compare with past operations
D. Compare with predictions of accomplishment

IV. WHERE FORECASTS FIT

Control is after-the-fact while forecasts are before. Forecasts and projections are important for setting objectives and formulating plans.

Information for aiming and planning does not have to be before-the-fact. It may be an after-the-fact analysis proving that a certain policy has been impolitic in its effect on the relation of the company or department with customer, employee, taxpayer, or stockholder; or that a certain plan is no longer practical, or that a certain procedure is unworkable.

The prescription here certainly would not be in control (in these cases, control would simply bring operations into conformity with obsolete standards) but the establishment of new standards, a new policy, a new plan, and a new procedure to be controlled too.

Information is, of course, the basis for all communication in addition to furnishing evidence to management of the need for reconstructing the framework of management.

PROBLEM SOLVING

The accepted concept in modern management for problem solving is the utilization of the following steps:

A. Identify the problem
B. Gather data
C. List possible solutions
D. Test possible solutions
E. Select the best solution
F. Put the solution into actual practice

Occasions might arise where you would have to apply the second step of gathering data before completing the first step.

You might also find that it will be necessary to work on several steps at the same time.

I. IDENTIFY THE PROBLEM

Your first step is to define as precisely as possible the problem to be solved. While this may sound easy, it is often the most difficult part of the process.

It has been said of problem solving that you are halfway to the solution when you can write out a clear statement of the problem itself.

Our job now is to get below the surface manifestations of the trouble and pinpoint the problem. This is usually accomplished by a logical analysis, by going from the general to the particular; from the obvious to the not-so-obvious cause.

Let us say that production is behind schedule. WHY? Absenteeism is high. Now, is absenteeism the basic problem to be tackled, or is it merely a symptom of low morale among the workforce? Under these circumstances, you may decide that production is not the problem; the problem is *employee morale*.

In trying to define the problem, remember there is seldom one simple reason why production is lagging, or reports are late, etc.

Analysis usually leads to the discovery that an apparent problem is really made up of several subproblems which must be attacked separately.

Another way is to limit the problem, and thereby ease the task of finding a solution, and concentrate on the elements which are within the scope of your control.

When you have gone this far, write out a tentative statement of the problem to be solved.

II. GATHER DATA

In the second step, you must set out to collect all the information that might have a bearing on the problem. Do not settle for an assumption when reasonable fact and figures are available.

If you merely go through the motions of problem-solving, you will probably shortcut the information-gathering step. Therefore, do not stack the evidence by confining your research to your own preconceived ideas.

As you collect facts, organize them in some form that helps you make sense of them and spot possible relationships between them. For example, plotting cost per unit figures on a graph can be more meaningful than a long column of figures.

Evaluate each item as you go along. Is the source material absolutely, reliable, probably reliable, or not to be trusted.

One of the best methods for gathering data is to go out and look the situation over carefully. Talk to the people on the job who are most affected by this problem.

Always keep in mind that a primary source is usually better than a secondary source of information.

III. LIST POSSIBLE SOLUTIONS

This is the creative thinking step of problem solving. This is a good time to bring into play whatever techniques of group dynamics the agency or bureau might have developed for a joint attack on problems.

Now the important thing for you to do is: Keep an open mind. Let your imagination roam freely over the facts you have collected. Jot down every possible solution that occurs to you. Resist the temptation to evaluate various proposals as you go along. List seemingly absurd ideas along with more plausible ones. The more possibilities you list during this step, the less risk you will run of settling for merely a workable, rather than the best, solution.

Keep studying the data as long as there seems to be any chance of deriving additional ideas, solutions, explanations, or patterns from it.

IV. TEST POSSIBLE SOLUTIONS

Now you begin to evaluate the possible solutions. Take pains to be objective. Up to this point, you have suspended judgment but you might be tempted to select a solution you secretly favored all along and proclaim it as the best of the lot.

The secret of objectivity in this phase is to test the possible solutions separately, measuring each against a common yardstick. To make this yardstick try to enumerate as many specific criteria as you can think of. Criteria are best phrased as questions which you ask of each possible solution. They can be drawn from these general categories:

Suitability –	Will this solution do the job? Will it solve the problem completely or partially? Is it a permanent or a stopgap solution?
Feasibility -	Will this plan work in actual practice? Can we afford this approach? How much will it cost?
Acceptability -	Will the boss go along with the changes required in the plan? Are we trying to drive a tack with a sledge hammer?

V. SELECT THE BEST SOLUTION

This is the area of executive decision.

Occasionally, one clearly superior solution will stand out at the conclusion of the testing process. But often it is not that simple. You may find that no one solution has come through all the tests with flying colors.

You may also find that a proposal, which flunked miserably on one of the essential tests, racked up a very high score on others.

The best solution frequently will turn out to be a combination.

Try to arrange a marriage that will bring together the strong points of one possible solution with the particular virtues of another. The more skill and imagination that you apply, the greater is the likelihood that you will come out with a solution that is not merely adequate and workable, but is the best possible under the circumstances.

VI. PUT THE SOLUTION INTO ACTUAL PRACTICE

As every executive knows, a plan which works perfectly on paper may develop all sorts of bugs when put into actual practice.

Problem-solving does not stop with selecting the solution which looks best in theory. The next step is to put the chosen solution into action and watch the results. The results may point towards modifications.

If the problem disappears when you put your solution into effect, you know you have the right solution.

If it does not disappear, even after you have adjusted your plan to cover unforeseen difficulties that turned up in practice, work your way back through the problem-solving solutions.

> Would one of them have worked better?
> Did you overlook some vital piece of data which would have given you a different slant on the whole situation? Did you apply all necessary criteria in testing solutions? If no light dawns after this much rechecking, it is a pretty good bet that you defined the problem incorrectly in the first place.

You came up with the wrong solution because you tackled the wrong problem.

Thus, step six may become step one of a new problem-solving cycle.

COMMUNICATION

I. WHAT IS COMMUNICATION?

We communicate through writing, speaking, action, or inaction. In speaking to people face-to-face, there is opportunity to judge reactions and to adjust the message. This makes the supervisory chain one of the most, and in many instances the most, important channels of communication.

In an organization, communication means keeping employees informed about the organization's objectives, policies, problems, and progress. Communication is the free interchange of information, ideas, and desirable attitudes between and among employees and between employees and management.

II. WHY IS COMMUNICATION NEEDED?

A. People have certain social needs
B. Good communication is essential in meeting those social needs
C. While people have similar basic needs, at the same time they differ from each other
D. Communication must be adapted to these individual differences

An employee cannot do his best work unless he knows why he is doing it. If he has the feeling that he is being kept in the dark about what is going on, his enthusiasm and productivity suffer.

Effective communication is needed in an organization so that employees will understand what the organization is trying to accomplish; and how the work of one unit contributes to or affects the work of other units in the organization and other organizations.

III. HOW IS COMMUNICATION ACHIEVED?

Communication flows downward, upward, sideways.

A. Communication may come from top management down to employees. This is downward communication.

Some means of downward communication are:
1. Training (orientation, job instruction, supervision, public relations, etc.)
2. Conferences
3. Staff meetings
4. Policy statements
5. Bulletins
6. Newsletters
7. Memoranda
8. Circulation of important letters

In downward communication, it is important that employees be informed in advance of changes that will affect them.

B. Communications should also be developed so that the ideas, suggestions, and knowledge of employees will flow upward to top management.

Some means of upward communication are:
1. Personal discussion conferences
2. Committees
3. Memoranda
4. Employees suggestion program
5. Questionnaires to be filled in giving comments and suggestions about proposed actions that will affect field operations.

Upward communication requires that management be willing to listen, to accept, and to make changes when good ideas are present. Upward communication succeeds when there is no fear of punishment for speaking out or lack of interest at the top. Employees will share their knowledge and ideas with management when interest is shown and recognition is given.

C. The advantages of downward communication:
1. It enables the passing down of orders, policies, and plans necessary to the continued operation of the station.
2. By making information available, it diminishes the fears and suspicions which result from misinformation and misunderstanding.
3. It fosters the pride people want to have in their work when they are told of good work.
4. It improves the morale and stature of the individual to be *in the know.*

5. It helps employees to understand, accept, and cooperate with changes when they know about them in advance.

D. The advantages of upward communication:
   1. It enables the passing upward of information, attitudes, and feelings.
   2. It makes it easier to find out how ready people are to receive downward communication.
   3. It reveals the degree to which the downward communication is understood and accepted.
   4. It helps to satisfy the basic social needs.
   5. It stimulates employees to participate in the operation of their organization.
   6. It encourage employees to contribute ideas for improving the efficiency and economy of operations.
   7. It helps to solve problem situations before they reach the explosion point.

IV. WHY DOES COMMUNICATION FAIL?

A. The technical difficulties of conveying information clearly
B. The emotional content of communication which prevents complete transmission
C. The fact that there is a difference between what management needs to say, what it wants to day, and what it does say
D. The fact that there is a difference between what employees would like to say, what they think is profitable or safe to say, and what they do say

V. HOW TO IMPROVE COMMUNICATION

As a supervisor, you are a key figure in communication. To improve as a communicator, you should:

A. Know: Knowing your subordinates will help you to recognize and work with individual differences.
B. Like: If you like those who work for you and those for whom you work, this will foster the kind of friendly, warm, work atmosphere that will facilitate communication.
C. Trust: Showing a sincere desire to communicate will help to develop the mutual trust and confidence which are essential to the free flow of communication.
D. Tell: Tell your subordinates and superiors *what's doing.* Tell your subordinates *why* as well as *how.*
E. Listen: By listening, you help others to talk and you create good listeners. Don't forget that listening implies action.
F. Stimulate: Communication has to be stimulated and encouraged. Be receptive to ideas and suggestions and motivate your people so that each member of the team identifies himself with the job at hand.
G. Consult: The most effective way of consulting is to let your people participate, insofar as possible, in developing determinations which affect them or their work.

VI. HOW TO DETERMINE WHETHER YOU ARE GETTING ACROSS

A. Check to see that communication is received and understood
B. Judge this understanding by actions rather than words
C. Adapt or vary communication, when necessary
D. Remember that good communication cannot cure all problems

VII. THE KEY ATTITUDE

Try to see things from the other person's point of view. By doing this, you help to develop the permissive atmosphere and the shared confidence and understanding which are essential to effective two-way communication.

Communication is a two-way process:
A. The basic purpose of any communication is to get action.
B. The only way to get action is through acceptance.
C. In order to get acceptance, communication must be humanly satisfying as well as technically efficient.

HOW ORDERS AND INSTRUCTIONS SHOULD BE GIVEN

I. CHARACTERISTICS OF GOOD ORDERS AND INSTRUCTIONS

A. Clear
Orders should be definite as to
—What is to be done
—Who is to do it
—When it is to be done
—Where it is to be done
—How it is to be done

B. Concise
Avoid wordiness. Orders should be brief and to the point.

C. Timely
Instructions and orders should be sent out at the proper time and not too long in advance of expected performance.

D. Possibility of Performance
Orders should be feasible:
1. Investigate before giving orders
2. Consult those who are to carry out instructions before formulating and issuing them

E. Properly Directed
Give the orders to the people concerned. Do not send orders to people who are not concerned. People who continually receive instructions that are not applicable to them get in the habit of neglecting instructions generally.

F. Reviewed Before Issuance
Orders should be reviewed before issuance:
1. Test them by putting yourself in the position of the recipient
2. If they involve new procedures, have the persons who are to do the work review them for suggestions.

G. Reviewed After Issuance
Persons who receive orders should be allowed to raise questions and to point out unforeseen consequences of orders.

H. Coordinated
Orders should be coordinated so that work runs smoothly.

I. Courteous
Make a request rather than a demand. There is no need to continually call attention to the fact that you are the boss.

J. Recognizable as an Order
Be sure that the order is recognizable as such.

K. Complete
Be sure recipient has knowledge and experience sufficient to carry out order. Give illustrations and examples.

A DEPARTMENTAL PERSONNEL OFFICE IS RESPONSIBLE FOR THE FOLLOWING FUNCTIONS

1. Policy
2. Personnel Programs
3. Recruitment and Placement
4. Position Classification
5. Salary and Wage Administration
6. Employee performance Standards and Evaluation
7. Employee Relations
8. Disciplinary Actions and Separations
9. Health and Safety
10. Staff Training and Development
11. Personnel Records, Procedures, and Reports
12. Employee Services
13. Personnel Research

SUPERVISION

I. LEADERSHIP

All leadership is based essentially on authority. This comes from two sources: It is received from higher management or it is earned by the supervisor through his methods of supervision. Although effective leadership has always depended upon the leader's using his authority in such a way as to appeal successfully to the motives of the people supervised, the conditions for making this appeal are continually changing. The key to today's problem of leadership is flexibility and resourcefulness on the part of the leader in meeting changes in conditions as they occur.

Three basic approaches to leadership are generally recognized:

A. The Authoritarian Approach
1. The methods and techniques used in this approach emphasize the *I* in leadership and depend primarily on the formal authority of the leader. This authority is sometimes exercised in a hardboiled manner and sometimes in a benevolent

manner, but in either case the dominating role of the leader is reflected in the thinking, planning, and decisions of the group.

2. Group results are to a large degree dependent on close supervision by the leader. Usually, the individuals in the group will not show a high degree of initiative or acceptance of responsibility and their capacity to grow and develop probably will not be fully utilized. The group may react with resentment or submission, depending upon the manner and skill of the leader in using his authority.
3. This approach develops as a natural outgrowth of the authority that goes with the leader's job and his feeling of sole responsibility for getting the job done. It is relatively easy to use and does not require must resourcefulness.
4. The use of this approach is effective in times of emergencies, in meeting close deadline as a final resort, in settling some issues, in disciplinary matters, and with dependent individuals and groups.

B. The Laissez-Faire or Let 'em Alone Approach

1. This approach generally is characterized by an avoidance of leadership responsibility by the leader. The activities of the group depend largely on the choice of its members rather than the leader.
2. Group results probably will be poor. Generally, there will be disagreements over petty things, bickering, and confusion. Except for a few aggressive people, individuals will not show much initiative and growth and development will be retarded. There may be a tendency for informal leaders to take over leadership of the group.
3. This approach frequently results from the leader's dislike of responsibility, from his lack of confidence, from failure of other methods to work, from disappointment or criticism. It is usually the easiest of the three to use and requires both understanding and resourcefulness on the part of the leader.
4. This approach is occasionally useful and effective, particularly in forcing dependent individuals or groups to rely on themselves, to give someone a chance to save face by clearing his own difficulties, or when action should be delayed temporarily for good cause.

C. The Democratic Approach

1. The methods and techniques used in this approach emphasize the *we* in leadership and build up the responsibility of the group to attain its objectives. Reliance is placed largely on the earned authority of the leader.
2. Group results are likely to be good because most of the job motives of the people will be satisfied. Cooperation and teamwork, initiative, acceptance of responsibility, and the individual's capacity for growth probably will show a high degree of development.
3. This approach grows out of a desire or necessity of the leader to find ways to appeal effectively to the motivation of his group. It is the best approach to build up inside the person a strong desire to cooperate and apply himself to the job. It is the most difficult to develop, and requires both understanding and resourcefulness on the part of the leader.
4. The value of this approach increases over a long period where sustained efficiency and development of people are important. It may not be fully effective in all situations, however, particularly when there is not sufficient time to use it properly or where quick decisions must be made.

All three approaches are used by most leaders and have a place in supervising people. The extent of their use varies with individual leaders, with some using one approach predominantly. The leader who uses these three approaches, and varies their use with time and circumstance, is probably the most effective. Leadership which is used predominantly with a democratic approach requires more resourcefulness on the part of the leader but offers the greatest possibilities in terms of teamwork and cooperation.

The one best way of developing democratic leadership is to provide a real sense of participation on the part of the group, since this satisfies most of the chief job motives. Although there are many ways of providing participation, consulting as frequently as possible with individuals and groups on things that affect them seems to offer the most in building cooperation and responsibility. Consultation takes different forms, but it is most constructive when people feel they are actually helping in finding the answers to the problems on the job.

There are some requirements of leaders in respect to human relations which should be considered in their selection and development. Generally, the leader should be interested in working with other people, emotionally stable, self-confident, and sensitive to the reactions of others. In addition, his viewpoint should be one of getting the job done through people who work cooperatively in response to his leadership. He should have a knowledge of individual and group behavior, but, most important of all, he should work to combine all of these requirements into a definite, practical skill in leadership.

II. NINE POINTS OF CONTRAST BETWEEN *BOSS* AND *LEADER*

A. The boss drives his men; the leader coaches them.
B. The boss depends on authority; the leader on good will.
C. The boss inspires fear; the leader inspires enthusiasm.
D. The boss says I; the leader says *We*.
E. The boss says *Get here on time*; the leader gets there ahead of time.
F. The boss fixes the blame for the breakdown; the leader fixes the breakdown.
G. The boss knows how it is done; the leader shows how.
H. The boss makes work a drudgery; the leader makes work a game.
I. The boss says *Go*; the leader says *Let's go.*

EMPLOYEE MORALE

Employee morale is the way employees feel about each other, the organization or unit in which they work, and the work they perform.

I. SOME WAYS TO DEVELOP AND MAINTAIN GOOD EMPLYEE MORALE

A. Give adequate credit and praise when due.
B. Recognize importance of all jobs and equalize load with proper assignments, always giving consideration to personality differences and abilities.
C. Welcome suggestions and do not have an *all-wise* attitude. Request employees' assistance in solving problems and use assistants when conducting group meetings on certain subjects.
D. Properly assign responsibilities and give adequate authority for fulfillment of such assignments.

E. Keep employees informed about matters that affect them.
F. Criticize and reprimand employees privately.
G. Be accessible and willing to listen.
H. Be fair.
I. Be alert to detect training possibilities so that you will not miss an opportunity to help each employee do a better job, and if possible with less effort on his part.
J. Set a good example.
K. Apply the golden rule.

II. SOME INDICATIONS OF GOOD MORALE

A. Good quality of work
B. Good quantity
C. Good attitude of employees
D. Good discipline
E. Teamwork
F. Good attendance
G. Employee participation

MOTIVATION

DRIVES

A drive, stated simply, is a desire or force which causes a person to do or say certain things. These are some of the most usual drives and some of their identifying characteristics recognizable in people motivated by such drives:

A. Security (desire to provide for the future)
Always on time for work
Works for the same employer for many years
Never takes unnecessary chances
Seldom resists doing what he is told

B. Recognition (desire to be rewarded for accomplishment)
Likes to be asked for his opinion
Becomes very disturbed when he makes a mistake
Does things to attract attention
Likes to see his name in print

C. Position (desire to hold certain status in relation to others)
Boasts about important people he knows
Wants to be known as a key man
Likes titles
Demands respect
Belongs to clubs, for prestige

D. Accomplishment (desire to get things done)
Complains when things are held up
Likes to do things that have tangible results
Never lies down on the job
Is proud of turning out good work

E. Companionship (desire to associate with other people)
Likes to work with others
Tells stories and jokes
Indulges in horseplay
Finds excuses to talk to others on the job

F. Possession (desire to collect and hoard objects)
Likes to collect things
Puts his name on things belonging to him
Insists on the same location

Supervisors may find that identifying the drives of employees is a helpful step toward motivating them to self-improvement and better job performance. For example: An employee's job performance is below average. His supervisor, having previously determined that the employee is motivated by a drive for security, suggests that taking training courses will help the employee to improve, advance, and earn more money. Since earning more money can be a step toward greater security, the employee's drive for security would motivate him to take the training suggested by the supervisor. In essence, this is the process of charting an employee's future course by using his motivating drives to positive advantage.

EMPLOYEE PARTICIPATION

I. WHAT IS PARTICIPATION

Employee participation is the employee's giving freely of his time, skill, and knowledge to an extent which cannot be obtained by demand.

II. WHY IS IT IMPORTANT?

The supervisor's responsibility is to get the job done through people. A good supervisor gets the job done through people who work willingly and well. The participation of employees is important because:

A. Employees develop a greater sense of responsibility when they share in working out operating plans and goals.
B. Participation provides greater opportunity and stimulation for employees to learn, and to develop their ability.
C. Participation sometimes provides better solutions to problems because such solutions may combine the experience and knowledge of interested employees who want the solutions to work.
D. An employee or group may offer a solution which the supervisor might hesitate to make for fear of demanding too much.

E. Since the group wants to make the solution work, they exert pressure in a constructive way on each other.
F. Participation usually results in reducing the need for close supervision.

II. HOW MAY SUPERVISORS OBTAIN IT?

Participation is encouraged when employees feel that they share some responsibility for the work and that their ideas are sincerely wanted and valued. Some ways of obtaining employee participation are:

A. Conduct orientation programs for new employees to inform them about the organization and their rights and responsibilities as employees.
B. Explain the aims and objectives of the agency. On a continuing basis, be sure that the employees know what these aims and objectives are.
C. Share job successes and responsibilities and give credit for success.
D. Consult with employees, both as individuals and in groups, about things that affect them.
E. Encourage suggestions for job improvements. Help employees to develop good suggestions. The suggestions can bring them recognition. The city's suggestion program offers additional encouragement through cash awards.

The supervisor who encourages employee participation is not surrendering his authority. He must still make decisions and initiate action, and he must continue to be ultimately responsible for the work of those he supervises. But, through employee participation, he is helping his group to develop greater ability and a sense of responsibility while getting the job done faster and better.

STEPS IN HANDLING A GRIEVANCE

1. Get the Facts
   a. Listen sympathetically
   b. Let him talk himself out
   c. Get his story straight
   d. Get his point of view
   e. Don't argue with him
   f. Give him plenty of time
   g. Conduct the interview privately
   h. Don't try to shift the blame or pass the buck

2. Consider the Facts
   a. Consider the employee's viewpoint
   b. How will the decision affect similar cases
   c. Consider each decision as a possible precedent
   d. Avoid snap judgments—don't jump to conclusions

3. Make or Get a Decision
   a. Frame an effective counter-proposal
   b. Make sure it is fair to all
   c. Have confidence in your judgment
   d. Be sure you can substantiate your decision

4. Notify the Employee of Your Decision
   Be sure he is told; try to convince him that the decision is fair and just.

5. Take Action When Needed and If Within Your Authority
   Otherwise, tell employee that the matter will be called to the attention of the proper person or that nothing can be done, and why it cannot.

6. Follow through to see that the desired result is achieved.

7. Record key facts concerning the complaint and the action taken.

8. Leave the way open to him to appeal your decision to a higher authority.

9. Report all grievances to your superior, whether they are appealed or not.

DISCIPLINE

Discipline is training that develops self-control, orderly conduct, and efficiency.

To discipline does not necessarily mean to punish.

To discipline does mean to train, to regulate, and to govern conduct.

I. THE DISCIPLINARY INTERVIEW

Most employees sincerely want to do what is expected of them. In other words, they are self-disciplined. Some employees, however, fail to observe established rules and standards, and disciplinary action by the supervisor is required.

The primary purpose of disciplinary action is to improve conduct without creating dissatisfaction, bitterness, or resentment in the process.

Constructive disciplinary action is more concerned with causes and explanations of breaches of conduct than with punishment. The disciplinary interview is held to get at the causes of apparent misbehavior and to motivate better performance in the future.

It is important that the interview be kept on an impersonal a basis as possible. If the supervisor lets the interview descend to the plane of an argument, it loses its effectiveness.

II. PLANNING THE INTERVIEW

Get all pertinent facts concerning the situation so that you can talk in specific terms to the employee.

Review the employee's record, appraisal ratings, etc.

Consider what you know about the temperament of the employee. Consider your attitude toward the employee. Remember that the primary requisite of disciplinary action is fairness.

Don't enter upon the interview when angry.

Schedule the interview for a place which is private and out of hearing of others.

III. CONDUCTING THE INTERVIEW

A. Make an effort to establish accord.
B. Question the employee about the apparent breach of discipline. Be sure that the question is not so worded as to be itself an accusation.
C. Give the employee a chance to tell his side of the story. Give him ample opportunity to talk.
D. Use understanding—listening except where it is necessary to ask a question or to point out some details of which the employee may not be aware. If the employee misrepresents facts, make a plain, accurate statement of the facts, but don't argue and don't engage in personal controversy.
E. Listen and try to understand the reasons for the employee's (mis)conduct. First of all, don't assume that there has been a breach of discipline. Evaluate the employee's reasons for his conduct in the light of his opinions and feelings concerning the consistency and reasonableness of the standards which he was expected to follow. Has the supervisor done his part in explaining the reasons for the rule? Was the employee's behavior unintentional or deliberate? Does he think he had real reasons for his actions? What new facts is he telling? Do the facts justify his actions? What causes, other than those mentioned, could have stimulated the behavior?
F. After listening to the employee's version of the situation, and if censure of his actions is warranted, the supervisor should proceed with whatever criticism is justified. Emphasis should be placed on future improvement rather than exclusively on the employee's failure to measure up to expected standards of job conduct.
G. Fit the criticism to the individual. With one employee, a word of correction may be all that is required.
H. Attempt to distinguish between unintentional error and deliberate misbehavior. An error due to ignorance requires training and not censure.
I. Administer criticism in a controlled, even tone of voice, never in anger. Make it clear that you are acting as an agent of the department. In general, criticism should refer to the job or the employee's actions and not to the person. Criticism of the employee's work is not an attack on the individual.
J. Be sure the interview does not destroy the employee's self-confidence. Mention his good qualities and assure him that you feel confident that he can improve his performance.
K. Wherever possible, before the employee leaves the interview, satisfy him that the incident is closed, that nothing more will be said on the subject unless the offense is repeated.

www.ingramcontent.com/pod-product-compliance
Lightning Source LLC
Chambersburg PA
CBHW081947210125
20607CB00053B/1322
* 9 7 8 1 7 9 9 3 4 8 8 5 6 *